The *Essential*
Nettle, Dandelion,
Chickweed & Thistle

Johnny Jumbalaya

The Essential Nettle, Dandelion, Chickweed & Thistle Cookbook

Johnny Jumbalaya

First published in 2003 by Johnny Jumbalaya

ISBN 0 9544158 1 7

Support website:
www.countrylovers.co.uk/wildfoodjj

INTRODUCING THE 'Essentials'

The original 'Really Wild Food Guide' covered more than 150 edible wild plants and it seemed worthwhile to develop ways of cooking the FOUR basic weeds that just about EVERYONE should be able to find on their outdoor travels around Britain - nettles, dandelion, chickweed and thistles. Apart from a wish to give outdoors' people more power to their elbow when they need to live off the land this guide is also about exploring new tastes. The book should also appeal to rebels looking for an antidote to the world of sterile, pre-packed supermarket foodstuffs. Be inspired - throw off the yolk of treadmill cooking and look at new culinary adventures and taste combinations that defy the norm.

The emphasis of these recipes is generally on helping folks with limited cooking facilities - from a basic MSR burner or Uno gas ring to a small cooker in the back of a camper van, or even a log fire. Readers with catering degrees or at home in the kitchen will obviously be able to produce sophisticated variations of the recipes and add more exotic ingredients, but please bear with us. Ultimately, it is the author's opinion that wild food does not, and should not, have to be tasteless.

The book is set out so that each of the plant species has its own section of recipes with some preceding notes on general preparation requirements for the plant. Ingredient measurements are based on single portions as the author feels that the last thing any tired camper wants to face at the end of a day is calculate fractions of measurements written for two, three or more mouths. The 'Quick Herb Guide' and some notes on outdoors cooking have also been included from the original 'Really Wild Food Guide'.

As with all cooking in the field it is the landscape around you - and not the supermarket shelf - which ultimately determines what meals you can conjure from hedgerow ingredients. An ability to improvise helps, as does the assistance of spices and extras which make the dishes more interesting and palatable. If you are not familiar with the plants covered by the book it is best to use a botanical Field Guide until you can properly identify the species with certainty. There are potential lookalikes out there so please be safe about your foraging, and certainly never put any plant near your mouth that has not been properly identified with certainty. If you feel the risks of using wild plants as food are too great then put this book down and head for the supermarket. Wild foods are not for you.

Wild ingredients should only be harvested from safe stocks. Nettles collected from a quiet country lane will probably be fine but don't use plants from busy roadsides. Avoid those near landfill sites, evil looking lagoons and stagnant water, or gathering plants from fields and neighbouring borders that may have recently been sprayed with chemicals. Look for signs of chemical deposits on leaves, or wilted plants. Agricultural herbicides are often selective, so you may find all the thistles in a field are wilted, but the rest of the greenery looks lush and inviting. If it has been sprayed it certainly won't be. The same goes for any small game you acquire. Look for signs of any poison, particularly in forest areas where poisoned bait may have been laid down for squirrels. Certainly never eat any dead animal that you find lying on the ground. Something killed it – a disease, old age or poison – and it may well have been poisoned.

It should be pointed out that, technically, a growing plant is the property of the landowner and therefore subject to ordinary law, while there is legislation in place which makes it illegal to uproot 'any' wild plant without 'authorisation'. One doubts that a landowner would worry about your picking bothersome weeds from their land but you should, out of courtesy, ask if you want to enter a field or land. And the laws of trespass do apply despite moves on right to roam.

If you have a **medical condition** it is important to do some extra background research or seek medical advice on how the wild plants in the guide may affect you. If you do have a medical condition or are pregnant then wild foods are probably not a good choice ! Sorry. And in the interests of safety the author suggests that it is best not to feed wild plants to young children.

Before you eat any of the wild plants included here for the first time please test your tolerance [like many foodstuffs a few individuals may be allergic]. Just try a small pinch of the plant - raw or cooked depending on instructions - then wait for several hours to check your reaction. If you do have **any** adverse reaction avoid eating the plant.

Have lots of fun with the tastes and textures in this companion to the 'Really Wild Food Guide'. There is an awful lot you can do with a few handfuls of simple weeds and a little know-how. What's more, you'll rarely be short of a meal when that local village shop fails to open.

JJ - Summer 2003

e-mail: wildfoodjj@yahoo.co.uk

COMMON / STINGING NETTLE
Urtica dioica

There can be hardly anyone who has not encountered nettle stings during their life - particularly anyone who spends time in the outdoors.

Nettles have a long and varied history in food and medicine. In 1661 London diarist Samuel Pepys mentions enjoying nettle pudding. Some sources suggest that the Romans brought stinging nettles with them to Britain's shores to keep themselves warm by stinging the skin. Ouch! There seem to be varying interpretations as to where the word 'nettle' derives. One theory says that it is from 'naedl' an Anglo-Saxon word for needle, another that it comes from an old word meaning to twist. The generic *Urtica* comes from the Latin for 'I burn', *uro*. And no, that has nothing to do with a currency with a similar sounding name.

Long stems of older plants produce a fibre which has been used since the Bronze Age for making cloth or sacking. It is a good alternative to flax and the author remembers reading somewhere that towards the end of World War One the cloth used to make shirts for German soldiers contained large amounts of nettle fibre. And only recently fashion designers have again been experimenting with nettle fabrics.

Nettle has been cultivated commercially for the production of medicinal chlorophyll, and herbalists use a tea made from dried leaves.

Technically the plant belongs to the Urticaceae or Nettle family. It is dioecious [having male and female flowers on different plants], a perennial, grows from 30-180 cm tall, flowers from May to September, has creeping roots, pointed, deeply serrated, and opposite oval leaves, and usually likes soils rich in nitrogen and potassium.

Nettles contain vitamins A and C, and a variety of minerals. Constituents include histamine - a protective substance naturally occurring in the body, and perhaps one reason why nettle juice can relieve its stings and the plant is used in treating eczema. However, repeated stinging can cause a recurrent rash [*a good reason to wear gloves when harvesting nettles for consumption*], while potential contra-indications exist from the plant being diuretic, the older leaves laxative, and an indication that blood pressure and sugar may be lowered. For these reasons readers with a medical condition should probably therefore seek expert medical advice before eating nettles.

COMMON DANDELION
Taraxacum officinale

If the nearest you ever got to dandelions as a youngster was blowing the seeds off the 'clocks' be prepared for a shock when you take your first bite into a raw dandelion. It is BITTER, BITTER, BITTER. However, there are ways of dealing with that bitterness as you will discover later.

Dandelions have had a long use in herbal medicine but most readers will know of its human consumption from dandelion and burdock beer, or sometimes home-made wine made from the yellow flowers [which are delicately sweet before they fully open]. Its roots have been used for making a magenta dye, the flowers in Middle Eastern baking, while the Russians used a related dandelion to produce rubber in WW2. But then that nation seems to have a long history of overcoming the adversities of climate, terrain and terrible circumstances.

As a species taraxacum is incredibly complex, with over a thousand micro-species in Europe and more than 200 of these in Britain alone. The name dandelion is a corruption of the French name for the plant 'dents de lion' referring to the jagged leaves. Linnaeus called it leontodon after the Greek meaning 'lion's tooth', and it is sometimes referred to as dens leonis in older herbals.

Technically, dandelion belongs to the Compositae, is a perennial growing up to about 30 to 40 cm tall, and flowers between March and October. It has long taproots, a rosette of basal leaves, hollow flower stem often tinged with red, and flowers composed of over 200 florets. It grows almost anywhere but prefers nitrogen-rich soils.

The common dandelion contains vitamins B and C, provitamin A, and the bitter constituents taraxacin and taraxacerin which are what make the tongue curl. The leaves are strongly diuretic and mildly laxative, and have been used in herbal and dandelion beer. For these reasons readers with a medical condition should seek medical advice before consuming dandelion. One other possible contra-indication is that the plant - especially the flower stalks - contains a milky latex-like sap which can irritate some sensitive skins. The author has never had a problem with this but if you have sensitive skin it might be best to protect your hands when handling dandelion. Dandelion roots have been used as a coffee substitute when dried [the roots shrink considerably], then chopped and roasted.

CHICKWEED
Stellaria media

Virtually no corner of Britain is untouched by that sprawling little plant chickweed which is found almost all year round. Normally the only folks who really give chickweed a second glance are eagle-eyed gardeners since the plant spreads rapidly, requiring copious weeding.

The plant is weak and straggly and yet it has medicinal properties. Made into a poultice it was once used to help heal wounds, skin irritations and inflammation. In Culpepper's day it was '*boyled with Hogs-Greas*' to make an ointment, and one old herbal pronounces that '*the juice taken inwardly is good against the scurvy*'.

The Latin name for the plant, *Stellaria,* means 'little star' while *media* refers to 'middle', there being other chickweeds and related species.

Technically chickweed belongs to the Caryophyllaceae family and is an annual plant. With sprawling stems, sometimes up to 30 cm, it likes moist, disturbed, cultivated and waste ground. Flowering virtually all year round - hence its prolific spreading capacity - the soft green leaves are oval or elliptical and are placed in opposite pairs. Lower leaves are stalked while those at the upper part of the stems are not.

Chickweed contains calcium, potassium and saponins and has been used as a foodstuff by both man and beast, or rather chickens. Saponins, however, are potentially poisonous judging from what the author has managed to research on the internet, so it is perhaps advisable not to eat raw chickweed in very large quantities.

THISTLES
Cirsium spp. & Others

Setting out this short introduction on thistles posed a bit of a problem for the author since there are a whole variety of thistles, some of which are NOT edible. From research into foraging authorities the best choice appears to be to concentrate mainly on members of the *Cirsium* species commonly found in Britain - *arvense, palustre, vulgare, eriophorum, oleraceum* - and the Nodding and Cotton thistles. Sow-thistles, some of which are edible, are not covered since they don't represent what the author believes to be the conventional view of 'true' thistles - that is plants having blobby purple flowers and prickles - but more of that later.

As there are such a large number of plants in the group - the author has not managed to get his hands on all of them - they are listed overleaf in a tabular format. In fact, the author has only managed to use the creeping, marsh and spear thistles so readers will have to explore the remainder at their own discretion, though research into authorities on foraging suggests that 'parts' of these particular plants are edible.

At the start of the thistle recipe section you will find more specific details on which parts of these plants are claimed to be edible. The roots of many of them contain the plant starch inulin - a naturally occurring, insoluble, polyfructoside comprising linear chains of fructose. While there seems to be some research around suggesting that such compounds are good for humans you should also be aware that inulin is the same compound found in Jerusalem Artichokes and the roots of Chicory among others, which may cause flatulence in some folks' digestive systems. If you are out on the hills this may not worry you, but just be aware of that happy thought.

Thistles are largely ignored by everyone, except farmers who wage constant war on various species to eradicate them [occupiers of land are required by law to control the harmful weeds *C. arvense* and *vulgare*]. Yet in times past the fluffy down of some species has been used as a stuffing material and as tinder, the extracts of some species as curdling agents, oil extracted from the seeds, the petals of the cotton thistle used as a yellow food colouring. And there were you thinking that thistles were only beastly prickled things designed just to make picnics and country walks troublesome.

CREEPING / FIFID / CANADA THISTLE C. arvense	Perennial Fl. 6-9 To 150 cm	Common	Much branched, grooved stems not spiny or winged. Alternate leaves very spiny and sometimes hairy. Base of upper leaves clasp stem. Young leaves covered with short hairs. Mature leaves sometimes hairy, upper side dark-ish green, lower side lighter. Flower heads numerous but small, and without spines. Extensive taproots to 3m.
MARSH THISTLE C. palustre	Biennial / Perennial Fl. 8-10 30-150 cm	Common	Little-branched stems winged to top. End leaf lobe not distinct. Uppermost leaves white-downy. Flower heads smaller and more crowded.
SPEAR / BULL THISTLE C. vulgare	Biennial Fl. 7-10 30-180 cm	Common	Stem has wide and spiny wings right to the top. Short flower stalk. Spiny leaves with long yellow spine. Distinct end leaf lobe - narrow and spear shaped. Lower leaves have short stalk, upper ones join the wing and therefore absent. Leaf margins wavy. Upper leaf surface rough and hairy/spiny, lower soft hairs. Long taproot to 70cm. Forms winter rosette. Sometimes confused with Musk Thistle. Flowers - purple / pink / white.
WOOLLY THISTLE C. eriophorum	Biennial Fl. 6-9 To 150 cm	C & S Britain	Stems not spiny or winged. Leaves deep cut and spiny. Cottony heads with upward curving, prickly pointed bracts around flower head.
CABBAGE THISTLE C. oleraceum	Perennial Fl. 7-9 50-120 cm	Natural- ized	Upper leaves usually without lobes. Large yellow-white flower heads.
NODDING / MUSK THISTLE Carduus nutans	Biennial Fl. 5-8 30-120 cm	Most of Britain / Rare Scotland	Flower heads usually solitary. Flower buds upright, bend later. Spined bracts facing pointing towards flower top. Rosette often large. Alternate leafs, mature ones often hairless with long mid rib with little/no winging. Taproot usually hollow near crown.
COTTON / SCOTCH THISTLE Onopordum acanthium	Biennial Fl. 7-9 To 300 cm	Common	Spiny, broad winged stems to top. Lower leaf stalks short, upper absent and joined to wing. Stems and both sides of leaves cottony. Leaf lobes have strong spines. Broad flower heads. Rosette in first year.

Three other *Cirsium* species the author has come across - but can find no authoritative references on their edibility - are *C. rivulare*, or the Brook Thistle, *C. dissectum*, the Meadow Thistle, and the Dwarf Thistle, *C. acaule*.

9

C. rivulare is sometimes grown by British gardeners for its good looks but is a common field plant on continental Europe. The perennial *C. dissectum* has softly spiny leaf margins with white cottony leaf undersides, a smooth stalk below the purple flower heads and is found in the southern part of Britain. *C. acaule* is that ground-hugging thistle that always seems to be present when you want to sit on the grass.

That other *Cirsium* species are edible suggests that *rivulare*, *dissectum* and *acaule* are **perhaps** edible too, but only 'perhaps'. As this is unknown to the author at the moment, if you do decide to experiment you do so at your own risk. For your own safety please DO be cautious and measured in your experimentation. Be safe, not dead ! A message emphasised many times in 'The Really Wild Food Guide'.

As for the Cabbage Thistle this is a naturalized plant in Britain but is common to central Europe. However, its larger leaves frequently have much more of an edible surface area than the other thistles listed and are therefore worthy of cooking if you come across the plant.

One of the problems of identifying thistles is that during various stages of a plant's life it can look very much like another species. For example, the ground-hugging dwarf thistle only grows in a rosette form yet the spear, musk and cotton thistle all produce winter rosettes - sometimes very large in their physical spread. For the author one of the best times to use thistles is when they are at their rosette stage.

The non-traditional thistles that you may come across that have edible parts are the Milk Thistle / *Silybum marianum* [leaves, seeds, stems, roots], and the leaves of Prickly Sow-thistle / *Sonchus asper*, Smooth Sow-thistle / *S. oleraceus*, and Field Sow-thistle / *S. arvensis*.

ABOUT THE 'Essential' RECIPES

There is an obvious paradox in attempting to produce 100 new recipes for use by folks both in the field or backpacking and those in the warmth of a fully equipped kitchen, but equally you might be on-board a narrowboat or in a caravan. From the experiences of the 'Really Wild Food Guide', and knowing that folks with rucksacks simply DON'T DO measurements in the field, the emphasis has been on trying to provide a regime where measurements may largely be done by eye and experience. Similarly, recipe portions are based on the unit of one. Simply scale up for more mouths, as opposed to working out fractions of teaspoons and fluid ounces.

Neither is any apology made for using lots of spices and sweeteners, because the wild plants covered are sometimes bitter and frequently bland. Of course you are at liberty to simply boil your weeds to death, but in so doing render them tasteless, without nutritional value and turn them into a fine sludge. After a few days of such joyous fare it is likely that you will crave for sausages, baked beans and mash, and look upon anything with four legs or feathered wings with longing eyes. So combinations of dried spices, which can easily be carried, will make a world of difference to what you do with these humble weeds. Throughout the recipes you will find that when garlic is required there is a deliberate vagueness of the amounts required so that folks who love garlic can use as much as they feel inclined to add, while not alienating many people who find garlic loathsome. However, where garlic is specified the dish will benefit from its addition to the pot. If you know how to identify Jack-by-the-Hedge / Garlic Mustard [*Alliaria petiolata*], and Ramsons, try some of their young leaves at least once as garlic substitutes. If you do like the taste then you obviously have an alternative for garlic proper - although neither want to be cooked in the same way as garlic but added as whole or chopped leaves late in cooking [ramsons loose their flavour with heat and garlic mustard doesn't look very appealing when cooked].

Each plant recipe section elaborates on general preparation details and, rather than endlessly repeat 'parboil before use' or 'simmer roots first' for each and every recipe, the details in the relevant plant introductory pages should provide you with the basics of pre-preparing the plant ingredients ready for use. Once you are familiar with the way these four types of plant react to cooking and also taste you will be able to mix and match ingredients as you prefer.

As with the RWFG, items like 'butter and oil' are specified because this is likely to fit a wider range of outdoors circumstances. Readers working from home or with a good knowledge of food will obviously be able to do far more, and refine the basic recipes.... selecting more appropriate oils, adding ingredients such as fresh coriander and fenugreek to Indian-style recipes, handfuls of parsley, and so on. For all home gourmets it is rather assumed that you will be using freshly ground pepper and appreciate when to use white rather than the black variety. In the outdoors such matters do really not come into the cooking equation. What you have is what you go with.

The author is also very aware that the cream content used in a few recipes will be regarded as highly unhealthy by some folks and that he will no doubt be visited by the nutrition and diet police. However, when burning off calories in the outdoors the occasional treat of a high octane food can be welcome - especially when it is wet and cold, and you are feeling thoroughly dejected. Lean cuisine will just have to await your arrival back in civilisation. That said, a number of the recipes are specifically designed to provide a complete mixture of greens, protein and carbohydrates [carbs] for outdoors consumption.

At first glance many recipes may look vegetarian but in fact they generally form the basis of veggies to accompany meat in one form or other, but could form a veggie diet. The recipes also assume white long grain rice rather than wild or whole-grain rice which take longer to cook and are therefore generally inconvenient for the outdoors' cook.

It goes without saying that - depending on what the ingredient is - the recipes assume the ingredients have been washed, gutted, dressed, cleaned, peeled or cored ready for use, and are bug and disease free. The author also presumes the reader has some basic cooking skills, knows about run of the mill foodstuffs, and which end of a pan to hold on to. By that same token, the amount of many ingredients can be adapted to taste. This is not about manicured, slavish cooking-by-numbers food, but providing outdoors' cooks with ways of adapting the plants around them. Feel at liberty to add more of the things that you like and modify cooking procedures to suit.

Enough said, although one may reflect upon Jean-Paul Sartre's existentialist observation on human nature and apply it to food with the impish thought that 'Hell is other people's cooking'. All in jest but, thinking about it, maybe not in some instances ! Now, on with your own essential cooking adventures.....

'Essential' NETTLES

Common nettles don't present 'the hungry' with much of a problem, apart from their sting which can be painful in large doses; the moral of which must be to wear a pair of gloves or wrap something round your hand, and to keep those skinny knees covered. Do be aware, though, that persistent stinging by nettles may cause a recurrent skin rash.

Containing vitamins C and A, the leaves are the edible part of the plant [nowhere has the author encountered any reference to the roots being edible, nor has he tried eating them as yet], and can be found for the best part of the year in warmer corners of the country. The leaves are best in the early part of the year, particularly during spring, with the most tender ones being the new emerging growth up to three or four inches high. At this stage the stems and stalks are tender too and may also be consumed. The plants have little or no sting at this point either, developing that well-tested defensive system as they mature into summer.

As stinging nettles grow their stems become fibrous and harder while the leaves become tough and hairy, and by the end of the year quite gritty. Somewhere the author saw a reference to the gritty leaves being bad for the kidneys so perhaps best avoid eating those older ones late in the year to be on the safe side. That said, nettles which have been trampled down or cut back in the summer [be careful they have not been treated with herbicides !] generally produce a second growth later in the year and this can be harvested for consumption.

On more mature nettles select only the softer and paler leaves from the upper plant. Once nettles have flowered [bolted] the leaves are not worth picking.

For the kitchen, the author uses two means of tackling the leaves, particularly where whole tops of plants have been picked and the leaves still need to be separated from the stalks. Simply place the shoots in a bowl, pour boiling water over and allow to steep for a couple of minutes. This destroys the stings and allows the leaves to be handled without gloves. It also starts the cooking process. Alternatively, wear gloves and pick away. Generally the leaves are cooked like spinach - being wilted or boiled as required - but obviously not consumed raw in their mature state as spinach can be. Nettle leaves may also be frozen, or dried for later use.

PIGEON WITH NETTLES AND DANDELION

1-2 pigeons
Butter and oil
Salt and pepper
2-3 cups nettle leaves
1 cup dandelion leaves
1 small red onion or shallot - thinly sliced
1 garlic clove - whole
½ cup chicken or vegetable stock

This is a pot roast with strong flavours from the pigeon and also the dandelions with their bitter-ish edge. Portion-wise the author's feeling is that a hungry person really needs two pigeons as there is little meat on them. Where you see a reference to a 'small onion' in the rest of the recipes think of using something about the size of a golf ball.

- In a lidded casserole melt a knob of butter and a good slug of oil.
- Meanwhile season the pigeons then add to the casserole when hot.
- Brown pigeons all over then remove and set aside.

- Put the greens into the casserole along with the garlic clove and onion. • Cook over a medium heat until the nettle and dandelion leaves wilt and begin to soften. • Add seasoning, the stock, the browned pigeons and any cooking juices. • Cover the casserole and cook in a preheated hot oven for about 30 minutes or until tender.

VARIATIONS & ALTERNATIVES
No pigeon ? Then substitute in the following order - pheasant, duck, chicken.

SAUSAGE & NETTLE STEW

2-3 cups nettle leaves - young
Water or stock
Chorizo sausage
Black pudding
Potato - sliced or cubed
Garlic clove - chopped [to taste]
Paprika - pinches
Butter or oil

Ingredient measurements have been left deliberately vague knowing that some folks turn pale at the mere mention of black pudding and others sometimes find chorizo too spicy. However, the combination of the two works quite well with the greens. Just go with the flow of what you have, and enjoy.

• Spread the nettles around the bottom of an ovenproof dish or casserole with just enough water to submerge the them. • On top of the greens layer your sausages - sliced or cut into chunks. • If using garlic fry it with some paprika for a few minutes and when softened dot the mixture around the casserole dish [in the absence of garlic simply sprinkle paprika over the contents of the casserole].

• Cover, and either place in a moderate oven, or cook on the stove until the potatoes are tender.

ALTERNATIVES
Another taste combination you might like to try is black pudding and dandelions; adding pre-prepared leaves to the black pudding in the last stages of frying, then continuing to wilt the leaves at a lower heat. The savoury taste of the sausage helps take the edge off the dandelion's bitterness, and is quite a good way to introduce people to dandelion [assuming they like black pudding], and also accustom your own taste buds to dandelion.

CHICKEN & NETTLE PATATAS BRAVAS

1 chicken breast - whole or diced
Paprika
Garlic clove - finely chopped [to taste]
Butter or oil
Lemon juice

1 potato - sliced or cubed
Butter or oil
1 small onion - finely chopped
Ground cumin - pinches
Salt and pepper
2-3 cups nettle leaves - young

One supposes the Spanish do not use nettles in their PBs, but then we're not in Spain, are we ? As a thought, for a more gamey version use pigeon breasts, but you may need 2 or 3 per person.

• Parboil the potato until it begins to soften but is still firm, drain and dry. • Fry the onion and add the potato. • Fry for a couple of minutes at a moderate heat before adding ground cumin, seasoning and the nettle leaves. • Stir in the leaves and spread evenly around the pan. • Cook until they wilt and soften. • Cover, set aside and keep warm.

• For the chicken, dust the meat with a little paprika. • Fry the garlic gently until if softens then add the chicken to the pan and a squeeze of lemon juice. • Cook until done. • Serve with the nettle and potatoes.

VARIATIONS & ALTERNATIVES
A frequent replacement for cumin in patatas bravas are chilli powder and paprika which can be mixed with tomato sauce. Or try tomato purée plus the addition of a little light soy sauce.

NETTLE & POTATO CURRY

1 medium to large potato - cubed
1 carrot - sliced
2-3 cups nettles
Butter or oil
½ tsp. green Thai curry paste
½ tsp. grated ginger
½ cup coconut cream
1 lime
Salt and pepper

The previous patatas bravas recipe led to some further thoughts on the combination of nettles with potatoes and this was one outcome...

• Boil the potato pieces until just beginning to soften then remove from the heat. • Similarly cook the carrots. • Pour boiling water over the nettles and allow to steep for a couple of minutes. • Drain, squeeze out excess water, then set aside.

• Heat some oil in a skillet and cook the curry paste and ginger gently for a couple of minutes. • Stir in the coconut cream and allow to boil. • Add the vegetables and mix thoroughly. • Reduce the heat and cook for a further 3 to 4 minutes. • Add a squeeze of lime juice and seasoning and stir in. • Serve with a main meat dish or as a veggie dish.

ALTERNATIVES
A brief note on the coconut cream used in this recipe and elsewhere in the book. The author's preference is for coconut cream rather than coconut milk as he feels the cream provides a much richer and thicker texture to the sauce produced. He generally keeps a 'block' of creamed coconut handy rather than using the liquid cream sold in small cartons. This is often too thick and needs to be thinned and, once the pack is opened, has a limited life. Simply dissolve some 'solid' coconut cream in water to produce a consistency somewhere between single and double cream.

Coconut cream can usually be bought in 100g blocks and is easily carried in a rucksack; eliminating the wasted deadweight of tin cans and liquid. There are powdered coconut milk products around but the author's liking for these is strictly limited to looking at the colourful packaging on the supermarket shelf.

RABBIT & NETTLE PILAF

½-1 cup rabbit meat - cubed
1 small onion - sliced
Butter or oil
Garlic clove - pulped [to taste]
1 tsp. pulped ginger root
Ground coriander, chilli and curry powder - pinches
½-1 cup rice
1 tomato
Water or stock [preferred]
1-2 cups nettle leaves
Salt

What better way, assuming that you have a little time available, than to make a lovely pilaf out of that rabbit you acquired ?

• In a heavy-bottomed pan fry the rabbit at a moderate heat so that it is cooked through but not browned. • Remove from the pan with a slotted spoon and set aside.

• Put the onion into the same pan and fry until nicely browned. • Next, add garlic, ginger, pinches of the spices and salt. • Continue frying for a couple of minutes and then add the rice, rabbit meat, tomato and water [twice the volume of rice used]. • Stir, bring to the boil for a couple of minutes and then turn the heat right down. • Cover and cook for 10 to 12 minutes, giving the occasional stir to prevent sticking. • Then stir in the nettle leaves [they will provide more moisture], cover again and continue cooking for about 5 more minutes then serve.

VARIATIONS & ALTERNATIVES
As a rabbit substitute try chicken, and chickweed for nettles.

NETTLE & PEANUT CHICKEN

1-2 cups nettles
1 ½ tbsp. peanut butter [coarse / unsweetened]
Salt and pepper
1 chicken breast
Lemon juice
½ cup coconut cream [see note page 17]
Water
Garlic clove - pulped [to taste]
Ground ginger, curry powder, cayenne - pinches

Absolutely nuts. And that's just the chicken, never mind the cook !

• Pour boiling water over the nettle leaves and steep for 1 or 2 minutes.
• Drain and squeeze out excess water. • Add a little seasoning and half a tablespoon of the peanut butter, then set aside.

• Make a narrow incision from one end of the chicken breast and widen the pocket internally using fingers and the knife. • Stuff with the nettle mixture. • Drizzle a little lemon juice all over the outside of the chicken breast.

• Add a splash of hot water to some coconut cream in a bowl. • Add the crushed garlic, spices and remainder of the peanut butter. • Place the chicken in a lightly oiled baking dish and spoon over the sauce mixture making sure the chicken is fully coated.

• Cover with foil and bake in a moderately hot oven for about 15 to 20 minutes then remove the foil and continue baking for another 10 to 12 minutes, or until the chicken is cooked through and tender.

NETTLE MEATBALLS

1 cup minced meat - pork, lamb, beef or mixed
½ cup fresh breadcrumbs - soaked in milk
1-2 cups nettles - cooked and chopped
Salt and pepper
1 egg - beaten
Flour
Butter or oil

1 small onion - grated
Garlic clove - finely chopped [to taste]
1 tomato - chopped
1 large mushroom - chopped finely
Butter or oil
Water or stock - slug
Salt and pepper

The author vaguely remembers that the Swedes have a good angle on meatballs, but feels this is one version they are unlikely to have tried.

• Place the nettle leaves in a bowl and pour boiling water over.
• Allow to steep for several minutes then drain, squeeze out excess water and chop.

• Put the meat, breadcrumbs, nettles, egg and seasoning into a bowl and mix together well. • Form spoonfuls of the mixture into patties then coat in flour. • Heat some oil or butter in a skillet and fry the patties until nicely browned on both sides.

• A sauce is made from the other ingredients. • Gently fry until well softened - adding some water or stock to stop the mixture drying out. • Add the mushrooms in the last stages of cooking. • Serve this sauce over your nettle meatballs.

NETTLE & SMOKED FISH SAUCE

1 small onion - chopped
Butter or oil [oil preferred]
2-3 cups nettles - young
1 cup water
1 tbsp. peanut butter [coarse / unsweetened]
Cayenne pepper - pinch
Smoked fish - cooked and flaked

• In a pan fry the onion until softened then add the cayenne, nettle leaves, plus the peanut butter mixed with about a ½ cup of water. • Mix together then cover and cook for about 5 minutes at a moderate heat. • Stir from time to time to prevent sticking. • Add flaked fish on top of the mixture and the rest of the water. • Cover again and simmer for another 5 minutes. • Serve with potatoes or rice.

NETTLE DHAL

2-3 cups nettle leaves
1 small tomato - chopped
½ cup split yellow lentils
Butter or oil
Ginger root
Garlic [to taste]
1 small onion or shallot - chopped
Chilli powder and ground turmeric - pinches
Salt - pinch

• Soak the dry lentils for at least an hour. • Make a paste from a couple of slivers of root ginger and a piece of garlic. • Fry the onion until it begins to soften and add the garlic-ginger paste. • Continue cooking at a moderate heat for another couple of minutes, stirring to ensure the mixture does not burn [add a drop of water if it starts to stick to the pan]. • Add the chilli powder, turmeric and salt and continue cooking gently. • Next, stir in the nettle leaves and coat with the mixture. • Drain the lentils and add to the pan along with ½ cup of water. • Cover and cook until the lentils are cooked and almost dry - stirring from time to time. • Serve with rice or on its own.

NETTLEBURGERS #1

½ cup chickpeas - cooked
1-2 cups nettle leaves - young
1 small onion or shallot - finely chopped
Garlic clove - finely chopped [to taste]
Salt and pepper
Ground coriander and cayenne - pinches
½ cup couscous - cooked
1 egg - beaten
Butter or oil

Our American cousins seem to have monopolized the burger stakes worldwide, but it's unlikely that they will serve these burgers up over the counter. But then we Brits are much more adventurous these days when it comes to food, and there are lots of nettles out there begging to be eaten.

• Drain the chickpeas and mash, finely chop the nettle leaves and combine in a bowl with the onion, garlic, spices and seasoning. • Mix everything together well.

• Beat an egg then spread the couscous on a flat plate in readiness for coating the burgers [as if using breadcrumbs]. • Take spoonfuls of the mixture and form small patties. • Dip in the beaten egg and then roll in the couscous and place on a plate ready for cooking.

• Put some oil in a skillet and heat till the oil flows easily. • Cook the burgers for a couple of minutes on the first side, checking to see that the couscous is not burning [it's important to ensure the oil is hot enough to instantly seal the burger rather than be absorbed but not hot enough to burn]. • Turn over and repeat with the other side.

NETTLEBURGERS #2

2 cups nettle leaves - young
Water - splash
1 small onion - finely grated
1 large egg - beaten
Salt and pepper
Couscous - cooked & uncooked
Butter or oil

• Start by moistening about ½ cup of the couscous with boiling water and leave to absorb [it does not need to be fully hydrated since water will be absorbed from the nettles during the frying stage]. • Keep some of the couscous uncooked for later.

• Wilt the nettles in the tiniest splash of water - just enough to start the process. • When wilted remove from the heat and squeeze out as much excess moisture as possible.

• Chop the cooked nettles and place in a bowl with the grated onion, couscous, seasoning and half the beaten egg. • The remainder of the egg will be used for coating your nettleburgers.

• Mix everything together thoroughly then form spoonfuls of the mixture into patties. • Dip into beaten egg and then into uncooked couscous. • If at all possible place in a fridge for half an hour to firm up the mixture.

• Heat some butter or oil in a pan and shallow-fry the patties until nicely browned. Without the aid of refrigeration you will need to allow the first side of the burgers to cook for 2 to 3 minutes at a moderate heat until the structure has begin to 'set'.

VARIATIONS & ALTERNATIVES
There is no reason why some minced meat cannot be added to the mixture, or even nettles mixed with mince and turned into a nettle meatloaf - in which case you could add some crumbed bread for bulk.

NETTLE POLENTA CHIPS

Polenta - cooked and as coating
Nettles - young / chopped
Egg - beaten
Butter or oil

This rather unusual recipe can provide you with carbs and greens to go alongside a meat dish, or even as starchy sticks which can be dipped into a sauce. The initial idea came about as a way of making polenta more interesting because it can be dreadfully bland on its own.

Instead of breadcrumbs some of the dry cornmeal itself is used as a coating substitute. In initial trials of this recipe the author dipped the 'chips' in milk before coating, but found too much of the shallow frying oil was absorbed. Beaten egg seems to provide a better barrier, particularly if the chips are double-dipped in egg and meal. Not yet tried by the author is the thought that deep frying in hot oil might also be a much better option for quickly sealing the chips.

• Begin by finely chopping nettle leaves. • Next, make up some polenta following the instructions on the packet. • Once the polenta is almost cooked stir in the chopped nettle leaves and salt and pepper. • Continue heating until the polenta is fully cooked then turn out the mass onto a cold surface such as a large plate - or even the cleaned bonnet of a car ! • Smooth out so that the mass is slightly less than half an inch thick. • Allow to cool and solidify - the mass will feel a bit sort of rubbery to the touch but in fact is rather brittle and fragile. • The next stage involves cutting the polenta into 'chips' about half an inch wide and three-ish inches long.

• Meanwhile, put some of the cornmeal onto a flat dish, beat an egg, and put about ¼-inch of oil in a pan and heat until it is very hot. • Dip the chips first in the beaten egg then roll in the cornmeal and repeat once more. • Place in the oil in batches and fry for several minutes or until golden brown.

VARIATIONS & ALTERNATIVES
Something the author has experimented with is adding spices such as cayenne to the meal used in the coating procedure. Other curry-like combinations such as ground cumin and turmeric might make interesting alternatives.

NETTLE & LAMB SOUP

1 pint water
½-1 cup lamb meat - minced
2 cups nettle leaves
1 spring onion [or shallot] - chopped
Garlic clove - crushed [to taste]
Light soy sauce
Salt and pepper

'Mary had a little lamb...' with some nettle soup. If all you have to hand is a lamb chop, shred the meat and use that.

This is a clear soup, and the lamb could be replaced by pork or chicken.

• Bring the water to a boil in a pan and add the minced lamb. • Allow to come to a second boil and then cook at a rolling simmer for about 10 to 12 minutes. • Home cooks might like to remove the froth which forms for presentation purposes.

• Next, add the nettles, onion, garlic, soy sauce and seasoning.
• Reduce the heat and simmer for about another 10 minutes.

VARIATIONS & ALTERNATIVES
Other interesting combinations might be with venison or humble rabbit. In these cases there's also the thought that a squidge of tomato purée might be worth adding, or some sliced tomato.

NETTLE & FRESHWATER FISH SOUP

1 small onion or shallot - sliced finely
Butter or oil
Ground cumin and turmeric - pinches
1 cup chicken or fish stock
1-2 cups of nettle leaves - young
Freshwater fish - chunks
Salt and pepper

• Slice the onion and gently fry until it softens then add seasoning, and pinches of ground cumin and turmeric. • Cook for another minute. • Add stock, bring to boiling point and then simmer for a couple of minutes. • Add nettles and cook for another minute or so. • Next, add the chunks of fish. • Remaining cooking time will depend on size of fish pieces, but cook until the fish begins to flake, then serve.

SPICY NETTLE SOUP

1-2 cups nettle leaves - young
½ pint water or stock
Butter or oil
Cumin powder - pinch
Ginger root
Lemon juice
Salt and pepper

Readers with a blender may like to purée the nettle leaves after their initial cooking stage. For those of you in the outdoors, just chop the leaves very finely to start with.

• Chop the nettle leaves and slowly cook in the water until tender. • Remove from the heat [and blend if required]. • Take a few slivers of ginger root and crush into a paste [or finely grate]. • In a pan heat a little butter or oil and add your ginger paste, pinches of cumin and ground pepper, and salt. • Allow to cook for a minute then add the cooked nettles and a slug of lemon juice. • Continue cooking on a medium heat for about another 4 or 5 minutes then serve.

NETTLE & RICE DUMPLINGS

1 cup nettle leaves - chopped
Butter or oil
1 cup rice - cooked
1 egg
1 tbsp. plain flour
Water - or stock [chicken preferred]

One lives in wonderment at how dreadful and tasteless those school dumplings were. One can only assume that the cooks were re-trained mechanics, rocket scientists or maybe Egyptologists without a prune-like wrinkly pharaoh to poke at. Anyway, these dumplings are very mild flavoured to be sure - the intention is to provide you with a few carbs and greens - but you can always adulterate the mixture with some flavouring. But then these dumplings will go well with savoury or spicy dishes alike.

There are a couple of variations on cooking method for this depending on whether you are in the field or warm and comfy in your own kitchen.

• Wilt the nettles in a little butter or oil and then remove from the heat and squeeze out excess water with the back of a spoon.

The next stage is where you will want to adapt your preparation method...

• For the rice you can either blend in a processor along with the egg and flour, or finely chop or mash the rice with a fork and then mix in some beaten egg and the flour. • In both cases the next step is to mix in the nettle leaves and combine everything thoroughly.

• Bring some water - preferably laced with stock or some herbs - to the boil and spoon neat dollops of the mixture straight into the water. • Allow each to cook for 2 to 3 minutes then remove, drain and then serve with a main dish.

HOT NETTLE & VEGETABLE SOUP

1-2 cups nettle leaves - young
1 cup sweetcorn, carrot and peas - mixed
1 medium size potato - cubed
½ pint water or stock [beef, lamb or chicken preferred]
1 tomato - chopped
1 small onion or shallot - sliced finely
Garlic - pulped
1 small green chilli - seeded
Butter or oil
Salt [if not using stock]

This recipe is more for readers at home with access to traditional vegetable fare. If you, or your guinea pig diners, are new to eating nettles this recipe might be a way of introducing them gently - hidden among other veggies. Then you can inform your guests that they've consumed weeds from your cabbage patch; rescued from a potentially unhappy demise on the compost heap.

• Cut carrots and potatoes into small pieces and chop the tomato.
• Separately slice the onion, garlic to preferred taste, and the chilli pepper finely.

• Add potato, sweetcorn, carrot and peas to a pan containing water or stock. • Bring to the boil, cover and simmer until tender.

• Meanwhile paste the onion and garlic along with the tomato - a blender is great for this for folks with one handy - and then gently fry these for 1 or 2 minutes. • Add to the vegetable pan along with the chilli pepper and salt [If using stock then you may not want to add extra]. • Cook for a further 3 to 4 minutes and serve.

CRAYFISH AND NETTLE SOUP

1 handful crayfish - cooked
1-2 cups nettle leaves - young
1 small onion - finely chopped
1 cup fish or vegetable stock
Ground nutmeg - pinch
Salt and pepper

There you are sitting on the side of the riverbank having lured a few wild crayfish and what better way to prepare them than with a soup ? Remember, ONLY catch the signal crayfish and NOT our native white clawed species which is protected and under serious pressure from the foreign interlopers.

• To cook the crayfish drop them into boiling water, cook for 3 to 7 minutes depending on size, then shell. • To get at the meat - in the tail - allow the crayfish to cool then take hold of the head and end of the tail, twist in opposite directions and pull gently to separate. • Pinch the bottom of the tail with your fingers to loosen up the meat and extract the meat in one piece. • The dark vein you can see is the intestine and should be removed with a sharp knife tip and discarded. • Quickly rinse the meat and set aside. [If you have the time and energy put the shells into a pan with a cup of water, simmer, and use the liquor as the stock base for the next part of the recipe.]

• Meanwhile... put the nettle leaves into a pan of hot stock along with the sliced onion and a pinch of nutmeg. • Season [there may be enough salt in the stock if of a commercial variety and not your own home-made contribution as mentioned above] and bring to the boil. • Simmer for a few minutes before removing from the heat.

• Next... depending on whether you are in the wilds, or are experimenting at home and prefer smooth texture soups... slice the crayfish or keep whole then add to the nettle mixture. • If required blend, but in either case the soup should be cooked at a simmer for another 2 to 3 minutes. • Serve - and if you are feeling indulgent stir in a slug of cream.

VARIATIONS & ALTERNATIVES
As a substitute for the crayfish try prawns or shrimps. Or flake in some cooked trout.

NETTLE & APPLE SOUP

2 cups nettle leaves - young
1 medium-large cooking apple - peeled / sliced
Butter - or oil
1-2 tbsp. cream
½ pint vegetable stock
2 sage leaves

One doubts that our dear old friend Sir Isaac Newton would have imagined his apples were destined for soup. Funnily enough Samuel Pepys, who was tucking into nettle pudding back in the 17th century, was a contemporary of Newton.

Depending on your circumstances you may want to run this soup through a blender or simply keep it chunky. If the latter consider chopping the nettle leaves into smaller pieces.

• Put a chunk of butter in the bottom of a pan, melt and swirl around. • Add the sliced apple and nettle leaves and cover the pan. • Cook on a moderately low heat until the contents have begun to soften. • Stir in the vegetable stock, raise to a rolling simmer and cook for 10 to 15 minutes. • Remove from the heat.

• The next step is dependent on your choice of a smooth or chunky soup. • For blending, allow the mixture to cool, blend, and then return to the pan and add a couple of fresh sage leaves. • For a chunky soup allow the mixture to cool a bit then add sage. • In both cases stir in the cream and warm through.

VARIATIONS & ALTERNATIVES
In the absence of sage try adding a pinch of cinnamon to give the soup a spicy aromatic quality rather than being herb based. If using cinnamon it might be worth experimenting with coconut cream or milk as a replacement for the cream ingredient. Just a thought.

NETTLES WITH RAISINS

2-3 cups nettles leaves
Salt
Butter or oil
1 handful raisins - or to taste
Garlic clove - crushed [to taste]
Almonds or hazelnuts - chopped / crushed

It's amazin' what raisins can do....

• Begin by soaking the raisins in some warm water. • Then put the nettles into a pan with a knob of butter and a pinch of salt. • Cook gently until the nettles wilt. • Once the veggie is soft remove from the heat, drain, squeeze out excess water and set aside.

• Drain the raisins, pat dry and set aside. • Then gently fry the garlic until it begins to change colour. • Add the nettles and raisins and cook for another 4 to 5 minutes. • Add extra seasoning if required then serve.

VARIATONS & ALTERNATIVES
You might like to consider adding toasted pine nuts for a mediterranean feel to this dish. Add sultanas too if you like these. Another thought is a combination of nettles, apples and raisins with a pinch of cinnamon.

NETTLES AND PORT

1 bacon rasher
2-3 cups nettle leaves
Butter or oil
Ground nutmeg - pinch
1 handful mushrooms - sliced thinly
Plain flour - 2 pinches
White port
Cream

Of course one can get very squiffy on that luverly stuff known as port [more please Vicar !] and in this recipe the white variety - rather than the red - ensures that there isn't too much staining of the nettle leaves, although the mushrooms will tend to darken the dish. If you can find the paler oyster mushrooms then use these to try and keep the dish pale.

• Fry the bacon until crisp then crumble or chop finely and set aside.

• Place the nettle leaves in a pan with a small knob of butter and gently wilt [or simply pour boiling water over tender young leaves and allow to steep of a couple of minutes].

• If using boiling water drain the leaves and press with the back of a spoon to squeeze out excess water. • Add a knob of butter [if none used to wilt the leaves] nutmeg, mushrooms and bacon, then mix. • Cook for 2 to 3 minutes. • Sprinkle the flour over and add slugs of port and cream. • Stir together gently then place on a low heat and cook for several minutes to thicken up a little.

LAZY NETTLE CASSEROLE

3-4 cups nettles
1 small can mushroom soup
1 small onion or shallot - sliced
Butter or oil
Salt and pepper
Grated cheese [optional]

Let's face it, life is much simpler when food comes ready prepared, out of a can or pre-packed from a supermarket. So this is a token offering for the lazy slob in all of us.

• Wilt the nettle leaves [young stems also possible in this recipe] then drain and set aside.

• Fry the onion until it starts to soften. • Add the nettles to the pan, stir in and cook for a minute or two. • Stir in the mushroom soup gently, then pour the mixture into a lightly oiled ovenproof dish. • Sprinkle grated cheese over if required. • Place in a moderate oven and bake for about 15 to 20 minutes. • Serve with potatoes or rice.

NETTLE CASSEROLE #2

1 medium onion - chopped
Garlic clove - crushed [to taste]
Butter or oil
Ground turmeric, cumin, ginger, allspice - pinches
1 small can tomatoes - chopped
1 cup chickpeas - cooked
1 tbsp. raisins [or sultanas]
Salt and pepper
2-3 cups of nettle leaves

• In a small heavy-bottomed pan gently fry the onion until soft. • Stir in the garlic and spices, and cook for another couple of minutes. • Add the chickpeas, tomatoes, raisins and seasoning. • Bring to the boil and cook for a couple of minutes, then reduce to a gentle simmer and cover. • After about 10 minutes stir in the nettle leaves. • Cook slowly for about another 8 to 10 minutes [adding a splash of water to prevent the mixture drying out too much].

NETTLE & MUSHROOM FRITTATA

1 small onion - thinly sliced or grated
Butter or oil
1 handful mushrooms - sliced
2-3 cups nettle leaves
2 eggs - beaten
Salt and pepper
Cheese - grated [optional]

Another variation on the nettle and mushroom combination, this time with eggs. Again, the stalk material of very young nettles will not present a problem with this recipe.

• Pour boiling water over the young nettle leaves and allow to steep for several minutes. • Drain, squeeze out excess water and set aside.

• Fry the onions gently in a small skillet until they start to soften then add the mushrooms. • Cook until softened. • Add nettles and some seasoning to the mixture and continue cooking for another 2 to 3 minutes. • Add the beaten eggs and distribute through the mixture with a fork. • Cook gently until the egg has set. • If using grated cheese sprinkle some over the top and either place the skillet under a grill or in an oven to melt [make sure the pan's a metal handled one].

NETTLE RICE BAKE

1 cup rice - cooked
2-3 cups nettle leaves - roughly chopped
1 egg - beaten
1 small onion - chopped
1 tbsp. milk
Cheddar cheese - small cubes [optional]
Butter or oil

Continuing an egg theme with nettles but a simple way of using up any leftover rice.

• Lightly grease or oil a small ovenproof dish. • Mix the ingredients together in a bowl and then put into the ovenproof dish. • Place in a preheated moderate oven and bake for 20 to 25 minutes or until a knife inserted into the bake is clean when removed.

NETTLE PILAF

1 small onion - finely chopped / grated [optional]
1 small red pepper - chopped
Butter or oil
½ cup rice
Water - stock preferred
1 small tomato - seeded & chopped
1-2 cups nettle leaves - chopped
Salt and pepper

A simple recipe to mix your carbs and veggies. Adjust ingredient proportions as you wish. Onion is not a necessity.

• Fry the onion in a good slug of oil until it softens then add the chopped pepper to the pan and cook for another couple of minutes. • Add some rice to the pan and stir around to coat grains with oil. • Level the rice then add water or stock to just cover. • Bring to the boil then reduce the heat to a gentle simmer. • Cover and cook for about 7 or 8 minutes then stir in the chopped tomato, nettles and a little seasoning. • Mix well and continue cooking for about another 3 or 4 minutes or until the rice is just cooked.

SESAME NETTLES

2 cups nettle leaves - young
Sesame seeds - pinch / crushed
Salt
Garlic - pulped [to taste]
Lemon juice
Pitta bread [optional]

This is just a little culinary to experiment with and use as an accompaniment to a dish, or blended and treated like a dip - hence the pitta bread. For readers at home a pestle and mortar are ideal for making a paste of the sesame seeds, garlic and lemon juice. Readers in the outdoors will have to make do with whatever crushing method they can improvise. Cooking is such fun, isn't it ?

• Crush the sesame seeds and mix with garlic, salt and a slug of lemon juice [amount depending on whether you prefer more of a paste or a dressing].

• Steep the young nettles in boiling water for several minutes - or cook over a gentle heat until wilted. • Drain and squeeze out excess water. • While the nettles are still warm add your paste / dressing and mix thoroughly. • Allow the greens to rest for a minute or so to absorb the flavours then serve.

NETTLES WITH PEANUTS

1 tbsp. unsalted peanuts - crushed
2 cups nettles
Butter or oil
Salt

Whole peanuts are used here but you could just as easily reach for a coarse peanut butter off the shelf instead. Try with hazelnuts too.

• Crush whole peanuts and set aside. • Wilt the nettle leaves in a little butter or oil. • When softened add the ground peanuts, salt to taste and stir. • Cook over a low heat for several more minutes.

NETTLE, ONION & POTATO FRY-UP

1 potato - cooked / diced
1 medium onion - sliced
Butter or oil
Paprika
2-3 cups nettle leaves
Salt

A simple way to use up leftover boiled potatoes, and then add some greens to your carbs.

• In a skillet gently fry the onion till nicely browned. • Reduce the heat and stir in a pinch of paprika and the nettle leaves. • Gently wilt the nettles and when almost softened add a pinch of salt and the diced potato. • Gently stir everything together. • Turn down the heat even lower, cover, and cook for about 10 to 12 minutes making sure to stir from time to time.

VARIATIONS & ALTERNATIVES
If you like more spicy food why not replace the paprika with a pinch of cayenne ? The other thing one could perhaps do is turn the basic recipe into an alternative type of nettle bubble & squeak - dropping the onion and spice, and adding corned beef. However, unlike the cooked cabbage in B&S a version using nettles will need gentle frying since the leaves are more delicate and will scorch.

	WALNUT¹	SUNFLOWER¹	SOYBEAN	SESAME²	SAFFLOWER	RAPESEED	PECAN	PEANUT - DARK	PEANUT - LIGHT	OLIVE	MACADAMIA	HAZELNUT	GRAPESEED	COTTON SEED	CORN	AVOCADO	SWEET ALMOND	ALMOND
FRYING		•	•	•	•	•		•	•				•	•	•	•	•	
SALADS	•	•	•	•			•	•	•	•		•				•		
MAYO.		•												•				
MARINADE		•								•								
BAKING	•		•		•	•	•			•		•						•
VEGETABLES									•		•							•

¹ Not for deep frying. ² Quick to burn so add in last stages of cooking.

THE QUICK COOKING OIL GUIDE

FRIED NETTLE PANEER SALAD

½-1 cup nettle leaves - young
½ pint milk
½ tbsp. lemon juice
1 red pepper - sliced
1-2 tomatoes - sliced
Salad dressing [lemon & oil]
Salt and pepper
Butter or oil

Paneer is a traditional curdled cottage cheese made widely across India and in this case has some ground nettle leaves added which impart a slightly sweeter taste to the cheese - at least in the author's view.

Two other things about this recipe which combines a protein source with greens. First, that it is slightly time consuming and second, that it is not really an economical way of making cheese unless you have a friendly goat, or a farmer who will sell you milk over the farm gate. In the author's experience you will get about 2 tablespoons of paneer from a pint of milk. Anyway... on with the cheese-making.

• Very finely chop, or roughly blend, raw nettle leaves. You should have about a tablespoon of what looks like wet green tealeaves. • Put to one side.

• Put the milk in a pan and bring to the boil. • Add the nettles in the last moments before the milk rises. • As it does so add the lemon juice, then remove from the heat, stir the mixture and add a pinch of salt. • The curdling cheese will begin to separate out while the nettles will have had sufficient heat to cook them.

• Next, place a sieve somewhere that it can drain and line with a piece of muslin or similar material. • Pour the contents of the pan into the muslin and allow to drip through. A little prodding and extra squeezing may be needed to speed things up if you are in a hurry.

• When fully drained put the muslin on a cutting board or similar and gather all the curd into one mass before spreading out on the muslin in an even layer about half an inch thick. • Square up the edges and then fold the muslin over. • Place something flat on top and weight this down - something about the weight of a brick will be sufficient for a small amount of cheese. • Leave for an hour or so to set.

• Meanwhile... prepare a basic salad with the red pepper and tomato to which a little seasoning has been added. Just before serving dress with a little oil and lemon juice mixed together.

• Next, cut the solidified paneer into pieces about an inch long and fry gently in some butter or oil until the pieces just begin to take on a little brown colour. • Place the fried cheese on top of the salad as it is served.

SPICY NETTLE & PANEER

1-2 cups nettle leaves - young
Ginger root - pasted
Garlic - pasted [to taste]
1 small green chilli
2 tbsp. water
Paneer
1 small onion
Butter or oil
Ground cumin - pinch
Garam masala - pinch
Salt and pepper
1 bay leaf [optional]

• Chop the chilli, add to a little sliced root ginger and garlic, then make a paste from these. • Place in a pan with the water and nettle leaves. • Cook on a medium heat until the leaves begin to wilt then set aside.

• Cut the cheese into sugar lump size pieces and gently fry until they just begin to brown, then remove from the pan. • In a little more oil or butter fry the onion until it softens then add the spices, pepper and salt and cook for another 1 to 2 minutes. • Stir in the nettles, and then fold in the fried cheese. • Slide a bay leaf into the mixture, drizzle a little oil over then bake in a moderate over for 20 to 30 minutes.

NETTLE & CHICKWEED KEDGEREE

1 cup nettle leaves - young
1 handful chickweed - chopped
1 small onion - chopped
Butter or oil
Ground turmeric - pinch
1 cup cooked rice
1 hard-boiled egg - chopped
Salt and pepper
Cayenne or paprika [optional]

This is a fish-less version of kedgeree [and by that token not kedgeree at all, but the word provides an impression of what this recipe is about]. In any case, flaked fish can always be added to suit your circumstances. For something really unusual, some freshly caught and cooked freshwater crayfish would be a real treat.

• Begin by pouring boiling water over the nettle leaves and steeping for a few minutes. • Then drain, chop roughly and set aside. • Roughly chop the chickweed.

• Fry the onion until it softens. • Then stir in a pinch of turmeric and continue cooking for another minute. • Add the rice and chopped nettle, some seasoning, and the optional sprinkle of cayenne or paprika. • Continue cooking the mixture for a couple of minutes then add the egg and mix in. • Lastly stir in the chickweed and distribute throughout the rice. • Remove from the heat and allow to rest for a minute or so to wilt the chickweed.

The young leaves of pre-flowering **White Dead Nettle** [*Lamium album*], and those of the **Red Dead Nettle** [*Lamium purpereum*] are possible substitutes for stinging nettles but cooking times will have to be adjusted as, in the author's experience of red dead nettle, the leaves are much more tender to start with. White Dead Nettle leaves have a texture more like the real stinging version. As a precaution, test your tolerance to either of these before using in quantity.

'Essential' DANDELIONS

The author finds dandelions, even young ones, awfully bitter [to the point of being revolting] and has to treat them before they become tolerable as a vegetable. However, dandelion is such a common and abundant weed that any outdoors' cook in need of roots and greens cannot really dismiss the plant. Once suitably prepared they are perfectly fine but you need, by a bit of experimentation in the early days of handling dandelion, to establish your bitterness tolerance level.

For dandelion leaves the author has several methods of dealing with the bitter taste, depending on available time and the type of recipe...

The simplest method is to chop the leaves across their width into one inch pieces. If in a hurry, then pour boiling water over to leach out the bitter constituents. Steep for 5 minutes then repeat the process and, if necessary, repeat a third time. The hot water cooks the leaves too, consequently requiring little extra cooking. Even large old leaves can be dealt with successfully in this way. If you have lots of time on your hands, or need the leaves in an uncooked state, follow the same process but use cold or tepid water and soak for several hours or overnight.

For 'whole' leaves, follow a similar leaching process but either partly slit the main leaf rib or, again if you have time, make nicks in the rib with a sharp knife [a pretty time-consuming effort]. The other option is straight boiling of whole leaves but they tend not to survive vigorous boiling. Changes of gently *simmering* water reduce this degradation.

Dandelion lateral and taproots are bitter too. They are covered with a skin that is easily removed by scraping a sharp knife over the surface, or using a clean pad-like pan scrubber kept for the same purpose. Once cleaned the author tends to slit or sliver the roots to provide more surface area and then soak in hot water to remove the bitterness. Raw skinned roots tend to discolour in air - solved by immersion in water.

Those fortunate enough to be in one place for a period of time can cover growing dandelions with a light-tight box or blacked-out cloche. This produces pale creamy coloured leaves with much less bitterness.

For the adventurous, collect the seeds of the dandelion 'clocks' and rub between your fingers over a sieve to remove bits of parachute fluff, then sprout and use like cress or alfalfa. They take about two weeks to germinate in ideal conditions. Dandelion leaves do not freeze very well.

HOT SPICY CHICKEN & DANDELION

1-2 handfuls dandelion leaves
½ -1 cup diced chicken
1 lime
1 small onion
1 small green chilli - seeded
Butter or oil
Salt and pepper
Cream - optional

The slight bitterness left in the dandelion leaves after pre-treatment complements the overall spiciness of the dish.

• Remove excess stalk material from the dandelion leaves and steep in a bowl. • Meanwhile, place the chicken pieces in a bowl and squeeze the juice of a lime over. • Separately slice the onion and green chilli. • In a heavy-bottomed pan first fry the onions until they begin to soften then add the chilli. • Continue gently frying for a minute then remove from the pan and set aside.

• Discard the water steeping the leaves and replace with more boiling water. • Add a little more oil to the frying pan and fry off the chicken until lightly browned and cooked through. • Stir in the cooked onion and chilli and continue cooking for another minute.

• Drain the leaves and add in batches to the contents of the pan, mixing thoroughly but gently. • Add seasoning to taste. If you wish to add cream stir some in now, but the heat needs to be on low-medium to prevent the cream splitting. • Serve with rice.

VARIATIONS & ALTERNATIVES
There's absolutely no reason why you shouldn't increase the amount of lime juice or green chilli if you like these.

SPICED DANDELION & ORANGE RABBIT

1 rabbit fillet or sliced meat
Salt and pepper
Flour
Butter or oil
1 tsp. grated ginger
Mustard powder - pinch
2 tsp. sugar
1 cup orange juice
1-2 handfuls dandelion leaves
1 spring onion - thinly sliced

• Sprinkle salt and pepper over the rabbit and rub in. Leave for 20 to 30 minutes then dust the meat with flour.

• Fry the rabbit at a moderate heat until nicely browned [but for a minimum of 5 minutes] then remove from the pan and set aside.
• Put ginger into the pan and heat for a minute, stirring to prevent burning. • Mix in the mustard and sugar then the orange juice.
• Simmer until the sauce begins to become thicker. • Put rabbit back in the pan and simmer for about 7 or 8 minutes, then add the dandelion leaves and spring onion. • Cook for a further 2 to 3 minutes and then season. • Serve with rice.

DANDELION IN MANGO CHUTNEY

1 small onion - finely chopped / grated
Butter or oil
2-3 cups dandelion leaves
1 tbsp. mango chutney

• Pre-soak the dandelion leaves to remove bitterness. • Drain off the water and shake off excess water [the remaining residual water will assist cooking].

• Gently fry the onion until it has become very soft and almost a pulp.
• Add the leaves and stir. • Cover and cook slowly until the leaves are almost wilted then stir in the chutney and cook for a further 2 to 3 minutes. • Serve with potato or rice.

PHEASANT WITH DANDELION AND APPLE

1 pheasant breast
Butter or oil
1-2 rashers bacon - chopped
1 small onion or shallot
2 tsp. flour
1 bay leaf
1 cup stock - chicken or vegetable
½ cup cider - preferably dry
1 small orange - juiced
1-2 cups dandelion leaves - chopped
1 medium potato - diced
1 small cooking apple - sliced
Sour cream
Salt and pepper

Teaming up dandelion with one of the treats of country fare - pheasant; hopefully with a bird hung for two or three days to tenderise.

• Gently fry the pheasant meat until it is lightly browned then remove from the pan and set aside. • Add the bacon and onion to the pan and cook for a few minutes until the onion begins to soften. • Then add the flour, stir in and cook for a minute or two. • Add the stock, cider, orange juice, bay leaf and seasoning - adjust salt according to amount of bacon used.

• Bring pan contents to the boil, put the pheasant back in the pan then reduce heat to a gentle simmer. • Cover and cook until the pheasant is done - about 15 to 20 minutes at a low heat.

• Meanwhile.... Boil the potato pieces until they just become tender then remove from the heat but keep warmed. • In a separate pan place a knob of butter, pinch of pepper, the peeled and sliced apple, and chopped dandelion. • Cook until softened. • Add the potato, sour cream to taste and seasoning, and then gently mix together. • Serve alongside the pheasant.

LAYERED DANDELION & MEAT BAKE

1 cup rice - cooked
½ cup pork meat - cubed
½ cup bacon / gammon ham - chopped
2-3 cups dandelion leaves
1 small onion - finely chopped
Garlic - pulped [to taste]
½ cup sour cream
2 tbsp. milk
1 cup stock - vegetable or chicken
2 tsp. paprika
Salt and pepper

Who needs fancy names like 'fruits de la mer' or 'chicken a la king' when you can have good old dandelion and meat bake from an English hedgerow ?

• Pre-soak the dandelion leaves to remove some bitterness. • Separately fry the bacon till it crispens and the pork till gently browned all over. • Set aside. • Fry the onion and garlic - gently so as not to burn - then stir in 1 tsp. of paprika and continue heating for another minute. • Place all the above cooked ingredients in a bowl, add hot stock and mix.

• Place the drained dandelion leaves in the bottom of an ovenproof dish. • Add seasoning. • Cover the leaves with the onion and meat mixture and spread out evenly. • Repeat with the layer of cooked rice. • Mix the sour cream and milk and drizzle over the rice. • Sprinkle with the remainder of the paprika then place in an oven and bake for about 30 to 40 minutes in a moderate oven [add a little more stock or water if the bake seems to be drying out].

VARIATIONS
This recipe can, of course, be made with nettle leaves. And if you are not overly health-conscious why not try this with corned beef ?

DANDELION STUFFED TOMATOES

Dandelion leaves - chopped
Gammon ham
Butter or oil
Tomatoes - whole / seeded
Cheddar cheese
Pepper

Perhaps not a recipe you wish to carry out in the field since this one is a wee bit fiddly, but certainly one to introduce any friends to eating dandelion and the concept of wild foods. Good luck with your mission !

• Trim off stalk material then chop leaves roughly and steep in hot water.

• Meanwhile, dice ham into small pieces and gently fry until cooked through. Set aside. • Slice off the tops of whole tomatoes and scoop out the seeds and pulp.

• Drain the water off the chopped dandelion leaves and gently press to remove excess water trapped. • Add the ham chunks and mix through with a fork. • Add a little ground pepper - the ham should provide enough salt. • Fill the hollowed tomatoes with the mixture and then top with a small chunk of cheese. • Place in a moderately hot oven for about 15 minutes.

BALSAMIC DANDELION LEAVES

Butter or oil
Balsamic vinegar
1 small onion - sliced
Salt and pepper
1-2 cups dandelion leaves

• Fry the sliced onion in a good amount of butter or oil until it begins to caramelize. • Drain some soaked dandelion leaves - gently squeezing out excess water - and add to the pan with a good slug of vinegar. • Stir, cover and cook at a moderate heat until the leaves have wilted, stirring from time to time. • Add seasoning and serve.

DANDELION & FISH STUFFED POTATOES

Small-medium size potatoes
Butter or oil
Dandelion flowers [young] or leaves
Freshwater fish [pike, perch, trout] - cooked / flaked
Cayenne or paprika
Salt and pepper

Carbs, greens and protein...

• Select potatoes that are about 1½-2 inches in diameter, peel, and then hollow out a cavity [use the cored remainder for soup or another recipe calling for potato]. • Fry the potatoes, trying to get as much all round browning as possible then remove from the heat.

• Remove the outer sepals from the flowers and most of the base receptacle. • Stuff the potatoes with the flowers, flaked fish and a touch of seasoning, and place in a baking dish. • Dribble a bit of oil or smear with a dab of butter into each cavity, very lightly dust with cayenne or paprika and then bake in a moderate oven for about 10 to 20 minutes, or until the potatoes are cooked through. • In the absence of an oven the potatoes may also be lightly wrapped in foil and cooked on the embers of a campfire - but leave a gap in the foil for the steam to escape.

	BARBEL	BREAM	CARP	CHAR	CHUB	DACE	GRAYLING	GUDGEON	PERCH	PIKE	ROACH	RUDD	TENCH	TROUT	ZANDER
BAKE	•		•	•	•		•		•	•	•		•	•	•
BRAISE	•	•	•	•						•			•		
STEW			•										•		
STUFF				•					•	•			•		•
GRILL	•		•	•			•		•	•	•		•	•	•
DEEP FRY							•	•							
PAN FRY				•		•			•		•		•	•	
POACH	•			•					•	•					•
BBQ				•											
STOCK					•	•						•			
MINCE						•									

THINGS TO DO WITH YOUR FRESHWATER CATCH

47

DANDELION & ORANGE CURRY

2 handfuls dandelion leaves / roots
1 small onion
Cumin, turmeric and chilli powders - pinches
Butter or oil
1 orange
Water or stock
Yoghurt [or cream]
Salt and pepper

This is one of the author's favourite recipes in the book. Somehow the sweetness of the orange complements that hint of bitterness left in the dandelion leaves after their preparation.

• Place the dandelion leaves and stripped roots in a bowl and pour boiling water over. Allow to steep for about 5 minutes. Discard the water and repeat. Check taste and repeat one final time if still too bitter.
• Drain and set aside.

• Meanwhile... Slice the onion and lightly fry along with pinches of the spices. Set aside. • Peel and segment the orange keeping back a few segments to be added in the latter stages of cooking. Squeeze out any juice left in the pithy remains to add to the curry.

• Put the pan back on a medium heat and stir in the bulk of the orange segments and juice. • Add a little extra stock or water [about ½ cup]. • Simmer for a few minutes then add the dandelion, stirring the mixture gently. • Cook for another couple of minutes then stir in a good dollop of plain yoghurt and add the remaining orange segments. • Remove from the heat, season, and allow flavours to infuse. • Serve with rice or potatoes.

VARIATIONS & ALTERNATIVES
In the absence of yoghurt try a spot of cream - as happened in the case with the original preparation of this recipe. The curry can be thickened through the addition of potato or some other flour based thickener.

DANDELION PETAL COUSCOUS

½ cup dandelion flowers
½-1 cup couscous
Stock or water
Salt and pepper - optional
Oil or butter

Something to do with those springtime dandelion, and / or other seasonal flowers. Young dandelion flowers have a delicate sweetness [older ones become bitter] and this recipe offers an unusual side dish or addition to a main course.

• Soak the couscous with just enough hot stock to cover and allow to absorb. • Meanwhile, take *recently* opened dandelion flowers and remove the green sepals then slice across the base of the flower to release the petals from the receptacle. • Separate the petal bundles using your fingers, discarding any remaining green bits. • Fluff up the couscous with a fork and mix in the petals - rubbing in to break up and disperse any petals still bunched together. • Place in lightly oiled ramekins and press down. • Place in a moderate oven for 5 to 10 minutes then turn out.

ALTERNATIVES
Where older flowers are used [which may have a bitter edge] consider making up a spicy sweet sauce to accompany - simply made, when fruit is out of season, by reaching for a good quality blackberry or blackcurrant conserve and adding a little chilli. Cooked rice could replace couscous.

BAKED CREAMED DANDELION

1 small onion - finely chopped / grated
Butter or oil
1 tsp. flour
Salt and pepper
½ cup milk
1 egg - beaten or separated
Chilli sauce - splash [optional]
1-2 cups dandelion leaves

This recipe has two ways of dealing with the eggs depending on your level of hunger or sense of culinary adventure.

• Pre-soak the dandelion leaves to remove bitterness. • Gently fry the onion until it is softened then add seasoning and the flour. • Mix thoroughly together over the heat, then dribble in the milk - stirring continuously so that a smooth mixture develops. • Allow sauce to come to the boil and thicken. • Remove from the heat.

The next stage of the recipe depends on whether you want a quick and easy route or a more refined one.

• For quick requirements beat the egg, adding a drop of the chilli sauce if required. • Place the mixture back over a moderate heat and then stir in the egg a bit at a time and stirring continuously to prevent it turning to scrambled egg. • Take off the heat and stir in the dandelion leaves. • Pour the mixture into a lightly oiled ovenproof dish and place in a pre-heated moderate oven. • Bake for about 15 to 20 minutes.

• For the more refined version, also much lighter, the broken egg yolks are first added to the sauce mixture, then the dandelion leaves followed by the egg whites which are whisked and then folded in. • Similar baking time.

BASIC BÉCHAMEL SAUCE - universal base of many a sauce

• Put 2 level tablespoons of butter in a thick-based pan and melt at a medium heat. • Gradually stir in 2-3 tablespoons of flour - the amount depending on the sauce thickness required. • Keep the mixture cooking for a couple of minutes then add ½ pint of milk a bit at a time while continuing to stir. [A similar volume of liquid made up of cream or stock with the milk could be used.] • Raise the heat slightly and continue stirring until the sauce thickens. • If making something like a cheese sauce, the cheese would then be added with some seasoning, and cooking continued until the cheese has melted.

BRAMBLE & DANDELION COUSCOUS

1 small onion - finely chopped
Butter or oil
Chilli powder - pinch
1 handful blackberries
1-2 cups dandelion leaves
Salt and pepper
Couscous
Water or stock [preferred]

Among the many dry carbohydrate sources the outdoors' cook can carry with them couscous must rank among one of the simplest to prepare. While on its own bland and boring, the combination of spiced sweet blackberry and complementary bitter-ish taste of dandelion transforms the staple.

Make sure you pick nice and sweet blackberries to counteract the bitterness of the leaves and complement the chilli flavour.

• Fry the onion until softened and then stir in a pinch of chilli powder.
• Cook for another 1 to 2 minutes then add the blackberries. • Cook at a moderate heat, allowing the blackberries to break down. • Stir in the dandelion leaves and cook until wilted, adding a little seasoning towards the end.

• Meanwhile, pour boiling water or stock over the couscous, allow to absorb then fluff up with a fork. • Serve with the spicy blackberry-dandelion on top.

VARIATIONS & ALTERNATIVES
Try serving this alongside rabbit - particularly fried rabbit - or duck.

DANDELION AND PARMESAN TORTILLA

1-2 cups dandelion leaves - chopped
Ground nutmeg - large pinch
1-2 tbsp. parmesan cheese - grated
2 eggs
Butter or oil
Salt and pepper

• Soak the chopped dandelion leaves in hot water then drain and express as much excess water as possible. • Put in a bowl and add the ground nutmeg, grated parmesan and mix together. • Next, beat the eggs well and add to the bowl along with seasoning. • Stir thoroughly.

• In a small skillet heat some butter or oil and add the egg mixture. • Cook gently until the tortilla has almost set them take off the heat. • Place a plate on top of the skillet and flip the tortilla onto the plate, then slide back into the pan. • Cook the other side for 4 to 5 minutes, or until the tortilla is fully set. • Once cooked remove skillet from the heat and slide the tortilla onto a plate and allow to cool.

MUSHROOM, DANDELION & COCONUT RISOTTO

1 small onion or shallot - finely sliced
Garlic - pulped / finely chopped [to taste]
1 cup mushrooms - sliced
1 cup rice - cooked
½ cup water or stock [preferred]
1-2 cups dandelion leaves - chopped
1 cup coconut milk
Salt and pepper

Unlike other recipes in the book using coconut cream this one does need a thinner coconut milk since the risotto wants to be slightly moist.

• Gently fry the onion and a little garlic until softened, then add the mushrooms and cook for a further couple of minutes. • Add rice and water to the pan and cook for 2 to 3 minutes. • Add the dandelion leaves and coconut milk and cook on a moderate heat until nearly all the liquid has evaporated or been absorbed [the risotto should be 'slightly' moist]. • Season and serve.

QUICK CURRIED DANDELION SOUP

1-2 cups dandelion leaves - chopped small
Curry powder - good pinch
Butter or oil
1 small onion or shallot - finely chopped
1 cup water or vegetable stock
1 tbsp. plain yoghurt
Salt and pepper

For readers at home this soup can be put through a blender at the end rather than leaving the leaves whole.

• Gently fry the onion until soft, then add the curry powder. • Continue cooking for 1 to 2 minutes then add the stock. • Allow to come to the boil then simmer for 2 to 3 minutes. • Add the dandelion leaves and cook for about 3 to 4 minutes or until wilted. • Remove from the heat and force the leaves through a sieve with the back of a spoon. • Cook the liquid and leaf purée for another minute or two. • Remove from the heat, stir in some yoghurt and serve.

VARIATIONS
Why not try a dollop of sour cream instead of the yoghurt ?

DANDELION & MUSHROOM SALAD

Mushrooms - sliced or small whole
Dandelion leaf - finely chopped
Mayonnaise
Sour cream
Salt and pepper

A simple salad using a small amount of raw dandelion leaf to provide little packets of bitterness against the creamy dressing. Use a good mayonnaise rather than a vinegar-based salad cream.

• Put the mushrooms and about a tablespoon of chopped leaves in a bowl. • Mix mayonnaise and sour cream in a 1:2 ratio [or your preferred taste]. • Season then add to the contents of the bowl and mix thoroughly so that the mushrooms are well coated.

HAWTHORN & PICKLED DANDELION SALAD

Dandelion flower buds
Vinegar - white
Peppercorns
Hawthorn leaves - young
Honey
Light soy sauce

The buds and sprouting spring leaves of hawthorn are remarkably tasty although there is a slight hint of an after-taste which some may not like. Frothy young hawthorn leaves are bright green - unlike the darker shade of later months - and also very tender. Here the leaves are served as a salad with a light soy and honey dressing, and garnished with pickled dandelion buds as an alternative to capers. **DO NOT EAT HAWTHORN IF YOU SUFFER FROM CARDIAC OR CIRCULATORY DISORDERS.**

• To make the pickles take unopened dandelion flower buds and remove the green sepals and any attached stalk. • Wash, pat dry and put in a small bowl. • Boil some clear vinegar with a few black peppercorns added. • While hot pour over the buds and allow to cool [you may need put a cover on to keep the buds submerged]. • When cold bottle and place in a fridge. • Use within about a month.

DANDELION ALOO

Dandelion leaves
Potatoes
Water
Butter or oil
Onion - sliced

Garlic clove - chopped [to taste]
Ground coriander, paprika, cayenne - pinches
1-2 cardamom pods
Salt and pepper

• Cube the potatoes and place in a pan. • Cover with some warm water, bring to a rapid boil then simmer for 10 to 12 minutes, or until the potato pieces are tender. • Add pre-soaked dandelion leaves half way.

• In another pan heat butter or oil and fry the onion and garlic until softened, then add the spices. • Stir around then remove from the heat to add the drained potato and leaves. • Stir everything together gently so that the potatoes don't disintegrate, and add any seasoning at this stage. • Continue simmering gently until the whole mass has lost more water.

CASSAVA & DANDELION FLOWER CRÊPES

1 part cassava flour
2 parts milk
1 part egg - beaten
Salt
Dandelion flower petals
Lemon & honey or orange juice

The author has been experimenting with yam and cassava, but just what DO you do with that cassava flour bought in your local exotic shop ?

When cassava flour is mixed with water or milk and cooked it becomes very sticky, and almost has the colour of wallpaper paste as well. The proportions used are a good starting point for any experimentation and the resulting crêpe hasn't the least glue-like qualities, although you will notice a difference in the surface texture. The colour is paler too.

• The petals come from recently opened or just opening dandelion flowers. Remove the green sepals then slice across the base of the flower receptacle to release the petals. • Separate the petal bundles using your fingers, discarding any remaining green bits.

• In a bowl mix the cassava flour, milk and egg and whisk into a batter. • Leave for 10 minutes then stir in a good handful of dandelion petals and distribute evenly.

• In a skillet heat some oil until it is hot. • Spoon or pour in a dollop of the batter and swirl around to form a circular mass. • Cook for about 2 minutes on the first side until lightly browned, then turn over and cook the other side for a further 1 to 2 minutes. • Remove from the skillet, plate, sprinkle over some more petals and drizzle over some honey and lemon, or orange juice.

BASIC PANCAKE MIX

If you want to rustle up quick pancakes here's a very basic recipe:

1 cup flour, 1 large egg, 1 tsp. baking powder, 1 cup milk, salt - pinch, butter or oil for cooking.

• With the exception of the butter place all the ingredients into a bowl and mix into a smooth batter - a splash of clear honey will add a little sweetness. • Some cooks stir melted butter or oil into the mixture. • In any case pour the mixture into a lightly oiled frying pan. • Cook each side until lightly browned.

FOR YOUR NOTES

When trying one of the wild plants listed for the first time, try tasting just a small amount of the prepared plant to check your tolerance. If you have any bad or allergic reactions avoid any further consumption.

Never put any plant into your mouth unless absolutely 100% certain of its identification and edibility. Don't even consider 'pretty sure' as an option.

Only gather ingredients from uncontaminated sources and environments.

'Essential' CHICKWEED

How nice that at least one of the wild plants here does not require an acre of preparation notes.

Really chickweed is best for salads since it reduces to virtually nothing when cooked, although it is possibly best for individuals not to consume large amounts of chickweed since it contains saponins which are potentially toxic. However, the author has not suffered from consuming odd handfuls of chickweed, nor have many foragers going before, but the first time round check your own tolerance by nibbling a little bit raw or cooked [depending on the recipe] then waiting for a couple of hours to watch for signs of any adverse reaction. If you do have any bad reaction then do not further consume chickweed.

Young pre-flowering chickweed is the most tender and soft. Simply tear off the young shoots and their leaves [don't bother picking the tiny individual leaves] and use as the recipe requires. Once the plants have flowered they begin to get rather straggly and stalky, and in the author's humble opinion are best cooked. With chickweed being so prolific there is generally enough new growth available for the forager to choose fresh greens over older plants.

In the absence of chickweed the author would recommend using the cooked leaves of *Galium aparine* commonly known as cleavers or goosegrass. You will probably be familiar with the straggly plant as the one that seems to clutch at your clothes when walking through fields, and leaves small little sticky bobbles stuck to you. Goosegrass is good in the spring when the stems are about 12 to 18 inches long, and only the leaves are worth eating. In the author's opinion chewing at the square shaped stems is probably comparable to chewing a doormat - although he has no experience of eating the latter - so far ! There's no escaping that goosegrass stems ARE chewy and this applies even in young growth a few inches high. However, there is a window in springtime when the 1 to 2-inch leaves alone are tender when cooked [they do not really have much taste]. Enough can be quickly gathered for a portion once you get the hang of plucking 5 or 6 of the small leaves at a time. By summer the main leaf mid rib also begins to get chewy and therefore the leaves are really only useful as a survival green. Goosegrass leaves will freeze, but defrosted lose their turgidity and are really only suitable for adding to a soup.

BIRCH SAP & CHICKWEED RISOTTO

2½ cups birch sap
1 cup rice
1 small onion - finely chopped
Butter or oil
1-2 cups chickweed - roughly chopped
Salt [optional]

Birch sap has a pale straw colour to it and is collected by tapping the tree trunks during spring. It is a process a bit like collecting rubber tree latex except that a small hole is bored in the trunk rather than slashing a groove in it. The sap has a very mild taste which can be concentrated by boiling. Indeed, a more concentrated birch 'syrup' is made by reducing sap to about 1/20th of its volume. It is suggested that to enhance the sap flavour you also concentrate a few pints down to the 2 to 3 cups required for this recipe.

Only a small amount of onion is recommended as it will overpower the delicate sap flavour. If using salted butter you might not want to add more salt. Strictly speaking arborio rice is normally used for risotto but there's nothing wrong with using whatever white rice is to hand.

• Finely chop the onion and sweat in some oil until it begins to soften.
• Add the rice to the pan and stir, cooking for a couple more minutes.
• Then add the sap [there's slightly more liquid in this recipe than you might otherwise use when cooking rice as the risotto should have a slightly wet consistency]. • Heat until the sap boils and cook the rice for a couple of minutes before reducing the heat to a low simmer. • Stir from time to time and continue cooking until the rice has a 'bite'. • Remove from the heat then add the raw chickweed. • Distribute throughout and leave your risotto to rest for a couple of minutes - the residual heat softens the leaves. • Serve.

VARIATIONS & ALTERNATIVES
Any other edible tender spring green could replace the chickweed, and perhaps a spot of garlic too; but then you don't want to overpower the delicate sap flavour. Goosegrass leaves can substitute for chickweed [see note on previous page], and so might the first spring leaves of hawthorn [see HEALTH WARNING on page 54].

REDCURRANT RABBIT & STIR-FRIED CHICKWEED

Rabbit pieces
Flour / cornflour [optional]
1 orange juiced
2-3 tsp. redcurrant jelly
1 small spring onion - sliced
1 small lime - juiced
2-4 handfuls chickweed
Soy sauce - splash
Sesame oil - splash [optional]
Butter or oil

• Cut the rabbit into fork sized pieces. • Heat some butter or oil and fry the rabbit. • If using flour, dust first before frying. • Cook until nicely browned all over then remove and set aside. • Add the juice of an orange to the pan and stir around before adding redcurrant jelly. • Stir till this dissolves then put the rabbit meat back in the pan. • Turn down the heat to a gentle simmer, cover and cook until tender.

• Meanwhile... In a separate pan gently fry the spring onion then add a squeeze of lime juice. • Stir, then add the chickweed, a slug of soy sauce and, if you have some to hand, a slug of sesame oil for a more oriental / eastern taste. • Stir-fry until wilted. • Serve alongside the rabbit and rice or potatoes.

CHICKWEED & EGG SALAD

1 handful chickweed
1 egg - hardboiled
1 red shallot - thinly sliced
½ cup plain yoghurt
1 tbsp. hazelnuts - chopped
1 tbsp. oil [olive preferred]
Salt and pepper

• Slice the egg, and the shallot very thinly, then place in a bowl with the chickweed sprigs torn into smaller pieces and the nuts. • Mix up an emulsion of the yoghurt and oil and dribble over the contents of the bowl. • Add seasoning, mix everything together well and then serve.

SPICED COCONUT, PIKE & CHICKWEED

1 small onion
1 small red chilli
Garlic - crushed [to taste]
Butter or oil
1 tomato - sliced
1 tbsp. dessicated coconut
Ground coriander - pinch
Salt
Pike fillet
Water
Lime juice
2-3 handfuls chickweed

• Gently fry the chilli, onion and garlic for 2 to 3 minutes. • Stir in the tomato, coconut, coriander and salt. • Stir well and cook for another couple of minutes on a moderate heat. • Place the pike fillets on top of the mixture and spoon over some of the juices from the pan. • Cover and cook for about 5 minutes. • Push the pike gently to one side of the pan. • Add a splash of water, a squeeze of lime juice, and stir in the chickweed [being careful not to break up the fish]. • Cook for a further 2 to 3 minutes. • Serve with potatoes or rice.

STRAWBERRY & CHICKWEED SALAD

Chickweed
Strawberries
Oil
Cider or wine vinegar
Salt and pepper

• Tear the chickweed and place in a bowl with halved or sliced strawberries - sliced is better for a more thorough distribution.

• Keep back several strawberries. • Place these in a small bowl and crush with a fork to extract some juice. • Add slugs of vinegar and oil to make a dressing [1 part vinegar to 3-4 parts oil]. • Mix, add a little seasoning, then pour over the salad ingredients and toss.

CHICKWEED & BREAD TORTILLA

1 slice thin bread - diced
1-2 cups chickweed - roughly chopped
2 eggs - beaten
Salt and pepper
Butter or oil

The bread should preferably be a little dry but certainly not stale [it's a simple way of using close to pensionable bread].

• Beat the eggs in a bowl then add the chickweed. • Add seasoning, then the diced bread and mix together well. • In a skillet heat some butter or oil and add the egg mixture. • Cook gently until the tortilla has almost set then take off the heat. • Place a plate on top of the skillet and flip the tortilla onto the plate, then slide back into the pan. • Cook the other side for 4 to 5 minutes, or until the tortilla is fully set. • Once cooked remove skillet from the heat and slide the tortilla onto a plate and allow to cool.

CHICKWEED WITH CHICKPEAS

1 slice of bread - crust removed & cubed
Butter or oil
Garlic - finely chopped [to taste]
Ground cumin - large pinch
Vinegar - splash
1 cup chickpeas - cooked or canned
2-3 handfuls chickweed
Salt and pepper

The Middle East meets Mid Dorset, Mid Under-nether or wherever...

• Fry the bread pieces in a little oil until nicely browned. • Add finely chopped garlic to taste, and the cumin. • Cook for a couple of minutes making sure to stir so that the garlic doesn't burn. • Remove ingredients from the pan and crush in a mortar and pestle along with a splash of vinegar. • Put the resulting paste into the pan and add the chickpeas - make sure to drain first. • Cook for 2 to 3 minutes, then stir in the chickweed [keep any residual washing water on] and cook until it wilts.
• Season to taste and serve.

CHICKWEED & BEEF STOCK SOUP

3-4 handfuls chickweed
½ pint beef stock
3 tsp. butter
2 tsp. plain flour
Salt and pepper
Ground nutmeg - pinch
1 egg - hardboiled / sliced

The original 'Really Wild Food Guide' contained a recipe for dried nettle leaves with beef stock - which is still a very useful nutritional package. This recipe updates that one, using fresh greens, adding some spice and an extra source of protein - egg.

• Start by making a basic roux by melting the butter in a pan and stirring in flour and gently cooking until smooth. • Bit by bit add the hot beef stock and keep stirring to ensure a smooth consistency. • Raise the heat and cook for 3 or 4 minutes. • Add the chickweed, seasoning to taste and the nutmeg. • Stir thoroughly and cook at a gentle simmer for 3 to 4 minutes. • Meanwhile, slice the hardboiled egg and drop into the soup just before serving.

SPICY CHICKWEED RICE

1 cup rice - pre-cooked
Chilli powder & ground turmeric - pinches
1-2 cups chickweed
Salt and pepper
Oil

• Tear the chickweed into manageable pieces and then place in a pan with a little water and cook gently till wilted. Set aside. • Put a tiny amount of oil in the bottom of a second pan and smear around. • Place on a low heat, add pinches of the spices and the cooked rice. • Mix thoroughly and simply warm through. • Stir in the chickweed, season and continue to warm through for a couple of minutes.

CHICKWEED, BACON & STILTON SALAD

1-2 handfuls chickweed
Butter or oil
2 bacon rashers - chopped
1 slice bread - crust removed & cubed
White Stilton - cubed
Mustard powder - pinch
Lemon juice
Salt and pepper

• Place the washed chickweed in a bowl. • Fry the bacon until crisp then remove from the skillet and set aside. • In more oil or butter fry off the bread cubes until they are browned all over. • Set aside and keep warm.

• Make a salad dressing from a little oil, lemon juice and the mustard. • Add the fried bread and the cubed Stilton to the chickweed. • Drizzle the salad dressing over and toss. • Crumble the bacon over and serve.

VARIATIONS & ALTERNATIVES
Other cheeses can substitute for Stilton although that cheese has its distinctive taste, and the dressing can really be adapted to personal preference. As an alternative try sour cream instead of the traditional salad dressing.

CHICKWEED SALAD WITH TROUT & HORSERADISH

Trout flesh - cooked and flaked
1 tbsp. lemon juice
1 tsp. horseradish sauce
1 tbsp. cream
Salt and pepper
1-2 handfuls chickweed

• Place lemon juice in a bowl and mix in the horseradish followed by the cream. • Mix thoroughly and season. • Put the chickweed into a bowl and pour the dressing over and toss. • Add more seasoning to taste and gently mix in the flaked trout. • Serve.

CHICKWEED COLESLAW

1-2 handfuls chickweed
1 carrot - grated [optional]
1 spring onion - finely chopped
Vinegar
1-2 tbsp. sour cream
1 tsp. sugar [caster preferred]
Salt and pepper
Paprika - good pinch

Somewhere between reality and outrageously wild food there comes this *alternative* coleslaw. If you have previously read the 'Really Wild Food Guide', and know your wild plants, then you might like to try replacing carrot with finely shredded burdock or other wild rootstocks.

• Place all the ingredients, with the exception of the paprika, in a bowl and mix together well. • Sprinkle paprika over the top.

VARIATIONS & ALTERNATIVES
For more crunchiness you can always add the traditional coleslaw ingredients like sliced cabbage, or some chopped green pepper.

CHICKWEED & TOMATO SALAD

1-2 ripe tomatoes - sliced
1-2 handfuls chickweed - roughly chopped
1 green pepper - chopped
1 small red onion / shallot - thinly sliced
Garlic - crushed [to taste]
Vinegar
Sugar [caster preferred] - pinch
Oil
Salt and pepper

• Seed the pepper, chop and place in a bowl with the tomatoes, onion and chickweed. • Crush enough garlic to taste and mix with some vinegar, oil and a pinch of sugar to make a dressing [make sure the sugar dissolves and the dressing is not gritty]. • Pour over the contents of the salad and toss. • Season to taste and serve.

ORANGE AND CHICKWEED SALAD

1-2 handfuls chickweed
1 orange - peeled and segmented
Oil
Ground pepper

So simple, but out of simplicity comes one of the best....

• Tear the chickweed into manageable pieces and place in a bowl with the orange segments. • Squeeze any remaining juice from the orange pith. • Drizzle over a little olive oil - it really has to be for this salad - and season with pepper [the author prefers not to add salt to this one]. • Toss salad and serve.

ORIENTAL CHICKWEED SALAD

Chickweed
Bean sprouts
Bamboo shoot
Spring onion [optional]
Egg - hardboiled / sliced
Oil
Vinegar
Salt [optional]

There is a veritable medley of tastes that could be played with in this salad, even down to making a dressing with a little honey and light soy sauce. Try to use one of the better flavoured vinegars as opposed to a malt type. You may want to leave the salt out and simply go for the taste of the veggies. Just be adventurous and explore !

• Simply mix the salad vegetables in a bowl. • In a small bowl mix the oil and vinegar into a dressing, drizzle the dressing over the veggies, toss then serve.

VARIATIONS & ALTERNATIVES
In the absence of bean sprouts try sprouted alfalfa, dandelion or thistle. As a substitute for bamboo shoot consider shredded and soaked burdock root, or even slivers of thistle root suitably prepared. The addition of sesame seeds - toasted or not - would also add an extra hint of the Far East.

AVOCADO AND CHICKWEED SALAD

1 ripe avocado - sliced
1-2 handfuls chickweed
Lemon or grapefruit juice
Oil
Salt and pepper

Yup! Avocados don't grow in Britain's outdoors that is admitted, so this recipe is one for readers at home trying to encourage unbelievers to sample your weeds.

• Chop the chickweed and place in a bowl with pieces of sliced avocado. • Make a simple dressing with oil and lemon juice [if using grapefruit why not add grapefruit pieces to the salad too ?]. • Add some seasoning to the dressing and drizzle over the contents of the bowl. • Gently mix through and serve.

MANDARIN ORANGE CHICKWEED SALAD

Chickweed
Spring onion - slivers
Canned mandarin orange OR 2 satsumas
Flaked almonds
Oil

Mandarin orange segments grow in profusion on supermarket shelves so this is one for home consumption - unless you intend to carry a tin of mandarins with you in the wilds. On the other hand there's that odd satsuma secreted in your pocket, isn't there ?

This wee salad recipe can be adjusted to circumstances since opening a can of tinned mandarin oranges for one person might not be practical. Instead use real tangerines, clementines or satsumas as alternatives.

• Tear the chickweed and place in a bowl. • Slice the spring onion finely and add to the bowl. • Peel and segment the satsumas but keep half of one satsuma back. • Crush or mash this portion with a fork to extract the juice. • Add the juice to a little light oil in a cup and mix. • Pour over the contents of the bowl, toss, and finally sprinkle with the flaked almonds.

CHICKWEED WITH PEANUT DRESSING

1-2 handfuls chickweed
Peanuts - unsalted / shelled
Ground cinnamon, paprika & chilli powder - pinches
Salt
Oil

A pestle and mortar or a food blender are really required for this recipe.

• Place the raw chickweed in a bowl. • Next, grind the peanuts and spices together and add a pinch of salt. • Dribble a very little light olive oil [or other good salad oil] over the chickweed. • Scatter the peanut mixture over the greens, toss and serve.

VARIATIONS & ALTERNATIVES
Another replacement for chickweed in salads are the young budding leaves of hawthorn [see WARNING on p 54]. A frothy bright green, the leaves are tender when young but do have a faint hint of bitterness in them. However, a simple salad dressing does wonders to mask the taste.

CHICKWEED, APPLE & RAISIN SALAD

1 tbsp. raisins [or sultanas]
Water
1 apple - diced
Ground cinnamon - pinch
Butter or oil
1-2 handfuls chickweed

Apple and raisins, and apples and dates are taste combinations which are well suited to each other. So here is a simple spiced up version with some chickweed greens.

• Soak the raisins in hot water for about 10 minutes. • Heat a little butter in a skillet and gently warm through the apple pieces, adding a pinch of cinnamon.

• Put the chickweed in a bowl. • Drain the raisins and add. • Then add the apples and juices from the pan and mix everything thoroughly. • Serve with some couscous or rice perhaps.

FOR YOUR NOTES

When trying one of the wild plants listed for the first time, try tasting just a small amount of the prepared plant to check your tolerance. If you have any bad or allergic reactions avoid any further consumption.

Never put any plant into your mouth unless absolutely 100% certain of its identification and edibility. Don't even consider 'pretty sure' as an option.

Only gather ingredients from uncontaminated sources and environments.

'Essential' THISTLES

Thistles are time-consuming to prepare - more a labour of love than anything else - but if you want to experiment with wild foods then... Thistles also happen to be generally plentiful in the wilderness larder and therefore a handy ingredient. NOT all thistles ARE edible but parts of those listed overleaf, and mentioned in the Introduction, are generally accepted as 'edible' by authorities on foraging. *It's essential that ALL prickles are removed from thistles as they will do serious damage to your insides! And DO test your tolerance before eating in quantity.*

Unless you have a really large specimen, and by the same token older and potentially more bitter, thistle leaves really don't provide much in the way of greens after the prickles have been removed. However, that bitterness can be reduced through soaking and boiling. As the season goes on the thistle leaves and stems can take on bitterness [and also become tougher], so you may need to parboil before use. Simply adjust the recipes to suit the circumstances you face.

Neither is bitterness present in every part of thistle leaves. For example, in the winter rosette of the spear thistle the leaf green may be bitter-ish but the main leaf mid ribs are succulent and quite bland. The roots too, are bland.

The stems, stalks and roots of thistles seem generally to discolour once exposed to the air. So after peeling place in water, acidulated if possible, and keep the pieces submerged. For this reason the author finds that with thistle stems it is best to peel almost at the last moment and then slice off the darkened stem ends that were exposed to air.

As for thistle roots, these are really about adding texture since they are generally bland taste-wise, and are usually best before the plant flowers. Some survival experts quote thistle roots as being edible raw, however it is the author's opinion that for basic everyday eating they are best cooked. Experience seems to show that, like burdock root, they get tougher with a harsh boiling, but may be tenderised through simmering. Where used in combination with leaves the roots will need pre-preparing so that leaves don't turn to mush before the roots cook through.

The author has preferred ways of dealing with thistle roots. For main taproots, which can be a bit tough, slice thinly and then cut into julienne-type strips. With the larger rat's tail lateral roots, which generally seem to be more tender, slice along the length with a sharp knife before cooking. In both cases, scrape the skin or rind off the roots with a sharp knife - or something like a clean pan scrubber kept specifically for this miraculous culinary occasion.

	LEAF	STEMS & STALKS	ROOT	FLOWER & FLOWER PARTS	SEED
Creeping C. arvense	✔	✔	✔		
Spear C. vulgare	✔	✔	✔	FLOWER BUDS	ROASTED
Marsh C. palustre	✔	✔			
Cabbage C. oleraceum	✔		✔		
Woolly C. eriophorum	✔	✔		FLOWER BUDS	
Cotton Onopordum acanthium	✔	✔		PETALS	
Musk Carduus nutans		✔			

THE PRACTICALITIES...

Acquiring and preparing thistles for cooking is something of an art, and obviously not a subject found in normal cookbooks devoted to everyday wimps of the veggie world like cabbage and lettuce. You have to tackle your foe with determination, and the first thing to do is protect your hands with gloves and your arms. For harvesting, a spade and a good thick pair of garden or industrial gloves are pretty essential - but not always as you will see. For food preparation the suggestion is a slightly less thin pair of leather gloves which are pliable but thick enough the stop the spines. Do not even consider rubber washing-up gloves.

When stems only are required the author suggests that you do not cut the thistle down straight away, but instead work with the plant standing and cut away at the spiny leaves going from top to bottom. For those species which have spiny wings it is now a simple task to take a knife and run or scrape it down the stem to remove the vicious defences. Peel when you return to base to prevent discolouring.

The next stage is to peel the stem of its outer skin which can be done with a handy peeler if the stem is strong and large enough to be handled. Another, more delicate - and time-consuming - way, is to take a knife and fray or cut one end at an angle and then peel off the skin in strips.

With leaves of spear thistle winter rosettes it is possible to strip the thick basal leaves - more productive when 8+ inches long - in situ. Reach for the base of the leaf stem as close as you can to the crown of the plant. Gently rub the stem there between your fingers to break the grip of the downy sheathing covering the mid rib and - quite firmly but not tightly enough the break the leaf off - stroke / pull towards the end. Repeat a couple of times and you should end up with a bright green leaf rib that looks like a little mini celery stick. Working round the leaf rosette you should soon acquire enough veggie for one portion.

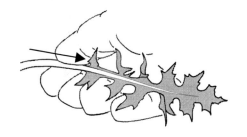

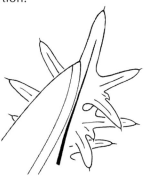

If you are working with 'pre-cut' thistle rosette leaves place each one on a chopping board and cut on either side of the main rib with a sharp knife. Just keep the thickest 3 or 4 inches of each rib and discard the rest of the greenery. Simply rub a sharp knife over the remaining leaf rib to scrape away any downy material to reveal the succulent green stem beneath.

The best advice for generally tackling thistle leaves is to begin by cutting off the tougher outer prickles of the larger leaf lobes with scissors [or a knife]. Once these more vicious spines have gone it is generally easier to deal with the smaller ones on the inner leaf curves and which can either be nipped out between your fingertips or with scissors. *And, as mentioned before, it is essential that ALL prickles are removed from thistles as they will damage your insides, and cooking will not soften them.*

The next stage of any preparation process is to check for the level of bitterness. Just break a tiny piece of the leaf off and crush it between your teeth and taste. If it is unpalatable then you will have to follow similar routines as with dandelions - soaking or boiling in several changes of water before use. Obviously soaking in hot water rather than boiling in a pan will better maintain leaf integrity, while chopping the leaves before soaking will provide more access to the leaf's cellular structure for the bitterness to be leached out.

Thistles are generally best before they 'bolt' [flower], but obviously if you were in survival mode.... In the past dried thistle roots have been ground and used as a flour addition - something not yet tried by the author. Another idea on the drawing board is to shred or grate thistle root and use in a burger or potato cake. The author did this with shredded burdock root mixed with potato mash and chunks of ham, then fried the patties. As a food the latter is a combination which provides fibre, carbs and protein.

AFRICAN STYLE RABBIT & THISTLE

1-2 cups thistle leaves / stalks
1 large tomato - skinned
1 tbsp. tomato paste
2 small onions - 1 sliced / 1 chopped
Cayenne pepper - large pinch
Oil - peanut for authenticity
Garlic - chopped [to taste]
1 cup rabbit meat - cubed
½ pint water
Salt and pepper
1 cup rice - pre-cooked

A hint of sub-Saharan cooking flavours here but reflecting ingredients to be found in the Britain's wilds. Originally the author used the leaf mid ribs of spear thistle winter rosettes for this recipe, but it could easily have been the peeled stalks of other thistle varieties like *C. arvense*, chopped into 1½ to 2-inch pieces depending on thickness and / or preference.

• Skin the tomato by making a nick in the skin and placing into boiling water for a minute or so. • Then remove the skin and place in a bowl with the tomato purée. Mash together and set aside.

• Next, gently fry the 'sliced' onion - so that it softens and browns. • Remove from the heat and place in a bowl [or mortar and pestle if working at home] along with the cayenne and pulverise.

• In a heavy-bottomed pan fry the 'chopped' onion and garlic [as usual the amount dependent on your personal taste] until they begin to brown. • Add the rabbit pieces and brown all over. • Add the pulverised onion-cayenne mixture, seasoning, thistles and water. • Raise heat till it begins to bubble then reduce to an oh-so-slow simmer, cover, and cook until the rabbit is tender. • Serve with potatoes, or perhaps with some boiled yam if you have access to this in one of our metropolitan centres, or rice.

VARIATIONS & ALTERNATIVES
Substitute chicken for rabbit, or lamb perhaps.

VENISON WITH THISTLE

1 cup venison - cubed
Butter or oil
1 small onion - chopped
Garlic clove - chopped [to taste]
1 small green chilli
1 cup thistle stalks / roots
2-3 tomatoes
Water [beef or vegetable stock preferred]
Salt and pepper

Once upon a time venison was the fare of royalty, their hanger's on and... outdoors' poachers of course ! Now, with more availability of venison, especially from estate managed resources, you too can live the life of kings... or a defiant poacher if you prefer.

• Seed and chop the chilli, onion and garlic. • Halve the tomatoes. • The thistle stalks should be peeled and cut into approximately 2-inch pieces and roots sliced then blanched in boiling water for 1 or 2 minutes.

• Cut the venison into 1-inch cubes and fry in a skillet until browned all over. • Remove venison and transfer pieces to a heavy-bottomed pan or casserole.

• In the residual frying oil fry the onion until softened, adding more oil if required. • Remove from the heat and add the onion to the casserole along with the garlic, chilli, tomatoes and thistle. • Stir the mixture well and season, then add water or stock [vegetable or beef best suited].

• Place casserole on the heat and raise to a very gentle simmer. • Cover and cook for 40 to 45 minutes, or until the venison is tender.

VARIATIONS & ALTERNATIVES
Beef would make a good alternative to the venison.

LAMB & THISTLE STEW

1 small or medium onion - sliced
Butter or oil
1 cup lamb meat - cubed
1 red chilli - seeded and chopped
Salt
1 tbsp. soft brown sugar
1 bay leaf
Water

1 cup thistle root - sliced
Ginger - grated [to taste]
Garlic - crushed [to taste]
1-2 tomatoes - sliced

A recipe for those not in a hurry...

• In the bottom of a small heavy-bottomed pan gently fry the onion until golden brown. • Raise to a medium heat and add the lamb. • Fry until the meat is nicely browned all over and sealed.

• Add the remaining ingredients [but not the thistle group of ingredients] and stir through before adding just enough water to reach the top level of the lamb. • Bring to the boil then cover and lower heat to a gentle simmer. • Cook slowly until the meat is tender, topping up with water if it begins to dry.

• Meanwhile... simmer the thistle root until just tender and set aside. • In a small pan gently cook the garlic and ginger and then add the tomato. • Cook for several minutes.

• Add the thistles and garlic-ginger-tomato mixture to the lamb and stir in. • Continue cooking slowly until a lot of the moisture has evaporated then serve.

WHOLE THISTLE & HAM SOUP

½ cup gammon or boiled ham - diced
1 small onion - chopped
1 carrot - sliced
1 cup thistle leaf
½ cup thistle roots
Rice [optional]
2 cloves
2 black peppercorns
½-1 pint water

The reason for the 'whole' in the title here is that every part of an edible thistle is a possible ingredient for this soup, but the rootstock needs tenderising before that part is added. The optional addition of rice is there to add a few extra carbs and thickening although you will need to add a little extra water to account for absorbtion. The ham should provide enough salt.

• Place all vegetable and ham ingredients in a pan with the water and add the spices. • Bring to the boil then cover and turn down the heat to a gentle simmer until the veggies are tender.

THISTLE & SAUSAGE CASSEROLE

1 cup mixed thistle stems and root - cooked
1-2 eggs - hardboiled
1 chorizo sausage
Butter or oil
1-2 tbsp. sour cream
Salt

• Cut thistle roots into slivers and simmer in water till tender. • Stems can be boiled until almost tender.

• Meanwhile slice the eggs. • Slice the chorizo and gently fry in a little butter or oil. • Place all the cooked ingredients in a small ovenproof dish. • Pour the sour cream over and place in a preheated moderate oven. • Bake for about 10 to 15 minutes.

THISTLE SOUP WITH PORK BELLY

1 slice pork belly
1 small onion
Garlic [optional]
½-1 pint water
1 cup thistle stem / root
1 carrot

1 dsp. butter
2 dsp. flour
1 tbsp. sour cream
Paprika - large pinch

Here any saltiness in the pork is a perfect way of enhancing potentially uninspiring thistle stems or roots.

• If using thistle stems make sure to peel and then cut into 1-inch pieces. • Thistle roots should first be cut into slivers or julienne matchsticks and then gently simmered until they start to tenderise.

• Slice the onion finely, and paste enough garlic to personal taste. • Place the pork belly, onion and garlic in the water, bring to the boil then cook slowly until the meat is tender. • Add the thistles and cook until tender.

• As the vegetables become tender prepare a roux from the flour and butter - melting the butter in a pan then gradually adding the flour and gently cooking until the mixture thickens. • Add the paprika and sour cream, stir briskly until smooth then add to the soup and stir in. • Bring to the boil. • Serve with the meat sliced into the soup.

LAMB & THISTLE SOUP

½-1 cup lamb - cubed
1 cup thistle stems
1 medium potato - diced
1 small onion - chopped
Butter and oil
Water
Paprika and ground caraway - good pinches
Salt and pepper
Sour cream

• Peel thistle stems and cut into 1 to 1½-inch pieces. • Cube the potato and chop the onion.

• In a pan fry the onion until it begins to soften then add the paprika and cook for another minute. • Then add the meat, seasoning, ground caraway and about 1 cup of water. • Cover and cook at a medium simmer. • When the meat is tender add the diced potato, thistle stalks and enough water to just cover. • Cook until the vegetables are tender then remove from the heat and stir in a good dollop of sour cream.

BASIC THISTLE SOUP

Thistle - leaf mid ribs / stems
Onion
Potato
Water / Milk - ½ pint per person
Butter or oil
Salt and pepper
Sugar to taste

Best with the youngest springtime thistle leaf mid ribs and foliage...

• Peel the onion and potato, and cut into small pieces. • Fry these and the thistle ribs gently until they begin to soften. • Then add a pinch of pepper and the milk or water. • Bring to the boil then cover and reduce to a simmer. • Cook until the vegetables are tender. • Add sugar and salt and serve. • Put through a blender if you have one handy.

PAPRIKA THISTLE SOUP

1 cup thistle leaf ribs, or whole 'prepared' leaves
½ pint water - chicken stock preferred
1 small onion - finely chopped
Oil or butter
Garlic - finely chopped
Paprika - large pinch
1 tsp. flour
1 tbsp. water
Salt and pepper
Vermicelli noodles [Italian pasta or even Chinese] - cooked

A lot of potentially exciting tastes and textures here... pasta for carbs, wild greens, and flavourings. And don't forget you can always add a handful of chickweed, or other wild greens if you have the knowledge of these.

• Simmer the thistle leaves or ribs in the stock until they start to tenderise but do not become fragile or soft.

• In another small pan gently cook the onion until softened and then the garlic for a few minutes. • Add the paprika and flour, stir, then dribble in a tablespoon of water and mix to form a smooth paste. • Add this paste to the main pan, raise the heat to allow the soup to thicken then add the cooked vermicelli noodles.

BASIC NOODLES & PASTA

For basic noodles which can be added to soup or stews... • Beat 1 egg with 2 tbsp. milk, and add a pinch of salt. • Add flour a bit at a time until a stiff dough is formed. • Flour a flat surface and knead the dough before rolling it out very thinly and cutting. • Depending on what you are preparing drop the pieces into boiling water, stock or bubbling stew. • Cover the pan and continue cooking for 15-20 minutes.

For pasta.... • For a more authentic pasta dough use a ratio of slightly less than 1 cup of a strong plain flour to 1 egg, just over 1 teaspoon of vegetable oil, and a pinch of salt. • Mix and cook in the same way above, although a lot of cooks like their pasta dough to 'rest' for an hour or so before use.

Unusual pasta doughs can be made with flours made from acorns or sweet chestnut meal [see the RWFG for more information]. Try making ravioli stuffed with nettles and cheese.

MUSTARD THISTLE LEAVES

1 cup thistle leaves - trimmed
Water
Salt
1 small onion - sliced
Butter or oil
Mustard powder - large pinch
1 dry red chilli - whole
Mild curry powder - pinch

1 tbsp. coconut - grated
Ground cumin and turmeric - pinches
Garlic clove - small piece
1 small green chilli

A great one for those succulent springtime thistle rosette leaves...
But also try with chickweed whilst amending the cooking times for that
gentle wild green.

• Make a paste out of the coconut, cumin, turmeric, garlic and green
chilli. • Place in a pan followed by the thistle leaves, a pinch of salt and
a ½ cup of water. • Cover and bring to the boil on a moderate heat then
remove from the heat and add another ½ cup of water. • Cover.

• Next, fry the onions until they are almost softened. • Add the mustard,
curry powder and dried chilli and continue cooking for another
1 to 2 minutes. • Add the mixture to the thistle leaves and fold in.
• Raise the heat and gently simmer until most of the water has
evaporated. • Stir occasionally to prevent sticking. • Serve with boiled
potato or rice.

SWEET CHILLI THISTLES

Thistle leaf mid ribs
Chilli powder - pinch
Oil
1 tbsp. tomato purée
Water or stock
Honey - clear
Salt and pepper

Another of the recipes cooked up with large mid ribs of winter leaf rosettes and great with something like shredded fried rabbit or sliced roasted duck.

• Drop the greens into boiling water and cook for about 3 to 5 minutes. Time will depend on rib thickness and bitterness [sample one rib after suggested time, however don't overcook].

• Meanwhile, take a pinch of chilli powder and heat in a pan with a slug of oil to release the flavour. • Add some tomato paste to the pan and stir in, followed by about 1 cup of water or stock. Stir. • Add the thistle greens and simmer gently for about 5 minutes. • Season to taste and then stir in a good slug of clear honey.

VARIATIONS & ALTERNATIVES
There's no reason why the leaf ribs could not be curried [add some diced potato for bulk], used as a simple vegetable, or perhaps boiled then added to a salad. Rather than using tomato paste you could use canned tomatoes to conjure a sort of vegetable stew. Serve alongside meat, or include meat within the recipe.

THISTLE STROGANOFF

Thistles - good handful leaves / roots
1 small onion or a shallot
½-1 garlic clove [optional]
Oil or butter
1 tsp. paprika
Water or stock
Cream
Salt and pepper

Who said food on the wild side was boring ? The idea of a thistle goulash did tempt the author's experimental curiosity but in the end this wild greens stroganoff was the one which got off the starting block. As the reader will be aware by now, preparing thistle leaves is a labour of love but in the author's opinion this was one recipe worth waiting for. No thistles to hand ? Then extend the stroganoff idea to chickweed with alterations to cooking time.

• Place the thistle leaves and roots in a pan with fresh water and bring to the boil. • Take off the heat and allow to steep in the hot water. Taste a bit of leaf for bitterness. If not to liking discard the water and repeat process, or pour in boiling water and steep again.

• Meanwhile... Slice the onions and crush the garlic. • Gently fry the onion and garlic until they become softened and lightly golden. • Reduce heat to a gentle simmer and stir in paprika and a little water or stock. • Cook for a couple of minutes.

• Drain water off the thistle leaves / roots and add these to the sauce. • Stir in some cream, season to taste, and continue to gently simmer for about 2 to 3 minutes [the cream will curdle if the heat is too high]. • Serve with potatoes, couscous or rice.

VARIATIONS & ALTERNATIVES
The ingredients call for garlic but that isn't essential if you don't have access. Possibly you could use wild garlic / ramsons, but the garlic flavour of that really tends to diminish when cooked.

THISTLE ROOT RAITA

½ cup thistle roots
1 tomato - seeded / chopped
1 small green chilli - finely chopped [optional]
1 spring onion [optional]
1 tbsp. plain yoghurt
Sugar - pinch
Salt and pepper

In case you were wondering what a raita is, it is a yoghurt side dish to accompany spicy dishes like curry.

• Slice the thistle roots into matchsticks and cut then across to produce small chunks. • Drop into some boiling water and cook until they just begin to get tender [the pieces want to have a bite to them]. • Drain and refresh in cold water. • Drain once more and pat dry. • Then simply place all the ingredients in a bowl - seasoning to taste - and just mix thoroughly.

THISTLE LEAF & MINT RAITA

Thistle leaf ribs - cleaned and finely chopped
1 small potato - boiled and cubed [optional]
Mint leaves - chopped finely
1 tbsp. plain yoghurt
1 small green chilli - chopped [optional]
Ground cumin - pinch
Salt and pepper

This is an even more cooling raita using mint and the succulent leaf mid ribs of thistle winter rosettes. Check that you like the taste of the leaf ribs before proceeding. They are not bitter but may not be to your liking.

• Chop the leaf ribs into small pieces and place in a bowl. • Slice and cut the boiled potato [firm and not mushy] into small cubes and add. • Mix the finely chopped mint into the yoghurt and then add this to the contents of the bowl, along with seasoning to taste and a pinch of cumin. • Mix everything together thoroughly.

STEAMED VANILLA THISTLES

Thistle stems - peeled and sliced
1 handful nettle leaves
1 vanilla pod or vanilla extract
Butter or oil
Salt and pepper

The inferior vanilla essence doesn't really do justice to this, so if you have the real thing....

• Cut the stems into 1 to 1½-inch pieces and drop into a little acidulated water to prevent discolouring.

• Meanwhile, put a piece of greased baking foil into the bottom of an ovenproof dish.

• Place the nettle leaves on the silver foil and the thistle stems on top of these [shake off as much water as possible]. • Scrape the vanilla seeds from the pod and distribute among the veggies. • Add several knobs of butter or drizzle some oil over. • Add a little seasoning. • Fold the kitchen foil up to make an envelope with crimped edges in which the stems and leaves will steam. • Place in a moderate oven for 15 to 20 minutes.

THISTLE WITH MUSTARD & HONEY GLAZE

Thistle roots - sliced thinly
Butter or oil
Salt and pepper
2-3 tsp. whole-grain mustard
1 tbsp. clear honey

• Take de-rinded thistle roots and cut into wafer-type slices. • Gently cook in water until they are just tender.

• Meanwhile... grease an ovenproof dish. • Then make a simple glaze by mixing the honey and mustard. • When the thistle is tender remove from the heat, drain and shake off excess water or pat dry. • Layer on the bottom of the ovenproof dish, season and brush liberally with the glaze. • Place in a hot oven and bake for 5 to 10 minutes.

THISTLE ROOT & CARROT SALAD

½-1 cup thistle root - julienne matchsticks / shredded
1 carrot - grated
1 tomato - sliced
1-2 handfuls chickweed [optional]
1 tbsp. clear honey
1 tbsp. plain yoghurt
Salt and pepper

• Cut the thistle root into matchsticks or slice into slivers. • Gently simmer in water until they have tenderised then refresh in cold water. • Drain off and place in a bowl. • Add the grated carrot, tomato, chickweed if used, and then season. • Mix the honey and yoghurt in a cup and then pour over the salad. • Mix together thoroughly.

SIMPLE BOMBAY THISTLES

1 cup thistle stems and roots
Butter or oil
Curry powder and turmeric - pinches
1 cup chicken or lamb stock
½ cup cream

Roots will need to be simmered prior to mixing with the stems for cooking but removed from the heat and refreshed with cold water before they become soft. Parboil thistle stems for a couple of minutes.

• Gently fry the thistles for several minutes. • Then add the spices and stock. • Bring to the boil then reduce heat to a gentle simmer and cook till the thistle is tender. • Remove from the heat and stir in a slug of cream. • Simply allow to the cream warm to through then serve.

VARIATIONS & ALTERNATIVES
Try using plain yoghurt as a replacement for the cream.

INDIAN THISTLES

½-1 cup thistle stems - chopped
Butter or oil
1 small green chilli
1 cardamom pod
1 clove
1 small piece cinnamon bark
Cumin seed - pinch
½-1 tsp. grated ginger
Garlic - ground [to taste]
1 small onion - finely chopped / grated
Ground coriander, chilli powder, garam masala - pinches
1-2 tomatoes - chopped
Water
Salt

This recipe has more than a hint of Indian cuisine. The amount of thistle and tomato may be varied depending on whether you prefer more thistle bulk or tomato.

• Peel the thistle stems and cut into fork sized pieces, then boil until just tender. • Drain, refresh with cold water and set aside.

• In a pan heat the cardamom pod, chilli, clove, cinnamon, cumin in some oil for a couple of minutes. • Add garlic and ginger and cook for another minute before adding the onion. • Continue cooking until the onion softens. • Add the ground coriander, chilli powder, garam masala and chopped tomato. • Stir and heat until the oil separates. • Mix in the thistle stems and add a splash of water. • Season, cover, turn down the heat low and simmer until most of the water is absorbed. • Serve with rice.

THISTLE BIRYANI

½ cup rice
1 cup water
Raisins and sultanas
1 cup thistle stems
1 small green chilli - sliced thinly
2 cloves
Ground cinnamon & caraway, mustard powder - 2 pinches
1 small onion - sliced thinly
Chilli powder - pinch
1 medium tomato
1 tbsp. yoghurt
Salt and pepper

If your local Indian takeaway manager has a sense of humour try asking him for thistle biryani next time you walk into his curry emporium.

• Cook the rice till just tender in a covered pan, and add a sprinkling of raisins and sultanas in the last few minutes and mix in. • Take off the heat and set aside.

• Peel thistle stems and cut into pieces about 1-inch long. • Parboil then fry them lightly in oil before removing from the oil and setting aside.

• Into the same pan place the green chilli, cloves, ground pepper, cinnamon, mustard and some pepper. • Gently fry for a minute keeping the spices stirred. • Add the sliced onion and continue frying until it starts to soften, then add a pinch of salt and chilli powder. • Add the tomatoes to the pan and cook till they are tender. • Add a dollop of yoghurt and mix through, then add the fried thistles, followed by the rice which should be gently folded in. • Cook for another 2 to 3 minutes or until everything is warmed through.

VARIATIONS & ALTERNATIVES
An interesting variation which begs investigation is the idea of replacing the raisins and sultana ingredients with dates, blocks of which are frequently carried by outdoors' folk. Somehow one thinks the caraway and cinnamon would disappear, and perhaps there be more emphasis on chilli or cayenne. Over to you and your sense of culinary adventure.

THISTLE & COCONUT CURRY

Butter or oil
1 small onion or shallot - chopped
1 small green chilli - sliced finely
Garlic - crushed [to taste]
Ginger root / grated - pinch
Ground cinnamon, turmeric, cardamom - pinches
1 ½ cups coconut cream [see note page 17]
Lemon peel - grated
1-2 cups of assorted thistle parts
1 small potato - diced

This is a great way of using rather tasteless thistle roots which have been cut into julienne-type strips or thin slivers, and other parts of the plant. Cardamom adds a more fragrant edge compared with the truer curry type of recipes. If you wish, double this spice proportionately to the others.

• Gently fry the onion, ginger, green chilli and garlic - if using. • Cook for several minutes then add the other spices and cook for another couple of minutes. • Add one cup of the coconut cream and a little grated lemon peel. • Gently simmer for 5 to 6 minutes then add the thistle. • Cook until tender then add the remainder of the coconut cream and cook for another few minutes.

CARAMELIZED THISTLES AND RED ONION

1 cup thistle root - sliced or julienne matchsticks
2-3 tsp. grated ginger
1 small red onion - rings
Butter or oil
Soya sauce
1 tbsp. clear honey

• Just tenderise the thistle roots gently by simmering in water then remove from the heat and drain. • Take the grated ginger and squeeze out the juice over the thistle roots. • Add all the other ingredients and mix together. • Place in an ovenproof dish and bake in a preheated moderately-hot oven until cooked and crisp-ish.

THISTLE, NETTLE & ALMONDS

1 small onion - sliced
1 tsp. grated ginger
Butter or oil
Ground coriander & turmeric - pinches
Salt and pepper
Mushrooms - sliced [optional]
1 cup thistle stems / leaf ribs - chopped
1-2 cups nettle leaves
1 handful almonds - flaked
Water
1-2 tbsp. plain yoghurt

Are you a nut freak ? Then add those wonderful almond textures and flavours to some of our readily available wild greens. Other woodland nuts like crushed hazels or beech masts are also a possibility but you may find that they are too assertive [thinking here of toasted beech masts which are very pungent].

The mushrooms are optional in the recipe as a means of bulking up the dish, but if using them you might want to add them to the pan before the nettles as mushrooms shed lots of water during cooking. Alternatively cut out some water and make use of the natural moisture in the mushrooms.

• Parboil thistle leaf ribs for 1 to 2 minutes and set aside. • Fry the onion and ginger. • When softened reduce the heat and add the spices and some pepper. • Drain the thistles and stir into the pan. Mushrooms should be added at this stage too. • Cook for several minutes, stirring gently. • Put the nettle leaves into the pan and a slug of water. • Reduce the heat and cook until the nettles have cooked and a lot of the water has been evaporated. • Season. • Fold in the flaked almonds and then the yoghurt. • Cook for a couple of more minutes and then serve.

TOMATO & COCONUT THISTLES

1 small onion - chopped
Butter or oil
1 cup thistle roots - matchsticks or thinly sliced
1 tomato - chopped
Ground turmeric and chilli powder - pinches
½ cup coconut cream [see note page 17]
Salt

• Gently simmer the thistle in water until it starts to soften then drain and set aside.

• Fry the onion gently until it softens and begins to turn a gold colour. • Add the thistle and tomato and stir thoroughly. • Add the spices and seasoning and cook for 3 to 4 minutes stirring occasionally. • Then add the coconut cream, reduce the heat to a low simmer and cook for another 4 to 5 minutes.

SPICY THISTLE RATATOUILLE

1 small onion - chopped
Garlic clove - chopped [to taste]
Oil
½ red chilli - seeded / chopped
1 cup thistle stems - peeled
1 small can plum tomatoes - chopped
1 courgette - sliced
Salt and pepper

• Begin by boiling the thistle stems for a couple of minutes then set aside. • Fry the onion and garlic [if using] for a couple of minutes until beginning to soften. • Add the chilli and cook for another minute, then add the tomatoes, thistle stems, courgette and some seasoning. • Simmer gently for 6 or 7 minutes, or until the veggies are tender but not mushy.

VARIATIONS & ALTERNATIVES
Red and green peppers can always be added to the mixture as in a more traditional ratatouille, and also aubergines.

STICKY TERIYAKI THISTLES

Thistle stems or roots
Oil
Soy sauce
Clear honey
Chilli powder / flakes - small pinch
Sesame seeds - optional

You may have heard of chicken teriyaki but here's the terrifying veggie version - eat your hearts out chicken lovers. If you have sesame seeds to hand add these to the teriyaki mixture for a slightly more authentic oriental taste.

• Lightly oil an ovenproof dish, or kitchen foil if using the foil envelope cooking method. • Mix the soy, honey and chilli. • Layer the thistle pieces in the ovenproof dish or place on foil, and then drizzle the teriyaki mixture over. • Place in a preheated hot oven and bake until the thistle is tender.

THISTLE & NETTLE SOUP

½-1 cup thistle stem / root - finely cut
Garlic clove - chopped [to taste]
Butter or oil
Tomato purée
1 cup vegetable stock
1 cup nettles - chopped
Pasta shapes - cooked
Parmesan - grated [optional]

This soup can be served as a coarse dish or run through a blender.

• Boil the thistle until just tender and set aside. • Gently fry a little garlic until it softens then add a squidge of tomato paste, stock, nettle leaves, and drained thistles. • Boil, then allow to simmer for 2 to 3 minutes.

• For smooth soup remove from the heat and allow to cool for a couple of minutes before running through a blender. • Then return to the pan.
• For either coarse or smooth soup the next step is to add the pre-cooked pasta shapes and warm through for 1 to 2 minutes. • Serve with grated parmesan.

CREAMED THISTLE SALAD & HAM

1 cup thistle roots / stems
1 small onion - finely chopped
2 eggs - hard-boiled / sliced
1 red pepper - diced
Cooked ham - diced
1 tbsp. sour cream
Vinegar
1 tsp. sugar
Salt and pepper
Paprika - pinch

• Simmer the thistles until tender then drain and refresh with cold water. • Place in bowl with the onion, egg, red pepper and ham. • Add sour cream, sugar, a slug of vinegar and salt. • Mix thoroughly and serve sprinkled with paprika.

THISTLES IN HAZELNUT SAUCE

1 cup thistle stalks / roots
1 small onion - finely chopped
Garlic - optional
Dried thyme, oregano - pinches
1 - 1½ cups stock - vegetable or chicken
½ cup ground hazelnuts [or peanuts or almonds]
2 tbsp. soured cream

• Put the thistles, onion, garlic, herbs and half of the stock in a heavy-bottomed pan. • Bring to the boil then reduce to a gentle low simmer. • Cover and cook until the thistles are tender. • Take some of the liquid and mix with the ground hazelnuts. • Stir this mixture thoroughly into the contents of the pan. • Add a little more stock now if you want a more liquid consistency. • Continue to cook for a couple of minutes before stirring in the sour cream. • Gently heat through then serve - as a vegetable dish with meat, or with rice or potatoes for a fully veggie outing.

THISTLE COLESLAW

½ cup thistle roots / stems
1 tbsp. mayonnaise
Vinegar - splash
Sugar - pinch
Salt and pepper
½ cup cabbage - shredded
1 apple - cored / diced

Now let's admit it, your average food guru is going to administer cabbage and carrot in coleslaw. But by this stage in the book we now know you're a food rebel. Well aren't you ?

Apart from the obvious mayonnaise aspect of coleslaw, 'crunchiness' of ingredients is key. Of the many wild plants available in Britain's outdoors the prepared roots of burdock will add a veggie with a great 'bite' - a bit like bamboo shoot.

• If using thistle roots cut into matchsticks and simmer for a few minutes. Drain and refresh with cold water. • For thistle stems cut into 1-inch pieces and boil until just becoming tender. Refresh with cold water.

• In a bowl mix the mayonnaise, vinegar, sugar and salt. • Add the cabbage, apple and thistle pieces which have been drained of the cold water and patted dry. • Mix everything together well.

BASIC VINAIGRETTE

This is the basic oil and vinegar salad dressing made by mixing 1 part vinegar with 3 or 4 parts of olive oil. Variously it may also contain some crushed garlic, herbs, seasoning, and even a spot of French mustard.

Simply place the ingredients together in a small bowl or cup, mix, drizzle over your salad then toss. If dealing with a bitter wild greens salad consider adding the juice of some freshly crushed raspberries or blackberries to the mixture to sweeten the dressing.

FOR YOUR NOTES

When trying one of the wild plants listed for the first time, try tasting just a small amount of the prepared plant to check your tolerance. If you have any bad or allergic reactions avoid any further consumption.

Never put any plant into your mouth unless absolutely 100% certain of its identification and edibility. Don't even consider 'pretty sure' as an option.

Only gather ingredients from uncontaminated sources and environments.

COOKING TEMPERATURE EQUIVALENTS

The aim of the guide has been to simplify the cooking process so readers without access to sophisticated equipment can feed themselves. For anyone happening to have access to more sophisticated technology in their narrowboat or camper van, the table below shows equivalent oven temperatures.

Gas Mark	Oven temperature	F° / C°
¼	Very Cool	225° / 110°
½		250° / 120°
1	Cool	275° / 140°
2		300° / 150°
3	Moderate	325° / 160°
4		350° / 180°
5	Moderately hot	375° / 190°
6		400° / 200°
7	Hot	425° / 220°
8		450° / 230°
9	Very hot	475° / 250°

THE QUICK HERB GUIDE

This quick guide shows which herbs can go well with meats, ingredients and dishes

	STOCK	SALADS	SOUPS	SAUCES	EGG DISHES	VEGETABLES	SAVOURY RICE	FISH	POULTRY & GAME	MEAT	FRUITS
ANGELICA											STEWED
BASIL		TOMATOES	✓	MILK	OMELETTES	MUSHROOMS	✓	FRIED	SHEPHERDS PIE	STEWS STEWS	
BAY	✓		✓	MILK		CAULIFLOWER		✓	✓		STEWED
BORAGE		✓	✓								
BURNET		✓	✓	MILK							
CARAWAY		✓	✓			CABBAGE / TURNIPS		✓		ROAST PORK	
CHERVIL		✓	✓	CREAM / EGG	✓	POTATOES / CARROTS		✓			
CHIVES		✓	✓			POTATOES					
CORIANDER		✓	✓	TOMATO		RICE		✓	CURRIES	CURRIES / STEWS	
DILL		CUCUMBER / DRESSINGS	✓	TOMATO	SCRAMBLED	POTATOES		✓		STEWS	
FENNEL		✓	FISH		✓	YOUNG VEG.		SALMON / MACKEREL	CHICKEN	PORK / VEAL	APPLE PIE
JUNIPER								✓	✓		
GARLIC	✓	✓	✓			CABBAGE		✓	✓		
LOVAGE	✓	✓	VEG	CREAM	OMELETTES	✓		✓	✓	STEWS	
MARJORAM		TOMATOES / DRESSINGS	✓		OMELETTES	✓		✓	STUFFING	STEWS	
MINT		✓	VEG / TOMATO	✓		POTATOES / PEAS	✓	✓	RABBIT	LAMB	FRUIT SALAD
OREGANO		DRESSINGS	✓	CREAM	OMELETTES	✓	✓	✓		STEAK	STEWED
PARSLEY	✓	DRESSINGS	✓	TOMATO	OMELETTES	✓	✓	✓	STUFFING	LAMB / STEWS	
ROSEMARY		✓	VEG		OMELETTES	TOMATOES		OILY FISH	CHICKEN	PORK / LAMB	
SAGE		✓	VEG		OMELETTES				GOOSE / DUCK	PORK	
SORREL		✓	✓					✓			
SWEET CICELY		✓	✓								STEWED
TARRAGON		TOMATOES / DRESSINGS	✓	CREAM / EGG	✓	✓		SHELLFISH	✓	VEAL	
THYME	✓	✓	✓	CREAM / TOMATO	BAKED EGG GRATIN	✓	✓	✓	STUFFING / RABBIT	STUFFING	